Pulse Of My Heart

A personal journey of ONE mind, heart & soul

R. L. WACHLIN

Order this book online at www.trafford.com
or email orders@trafford.com

Most Trafford titles are also available at major online book retailers.

Printed in the United States of America.

ISBN: 978-1-4269-9744-0 (sc)
ISBN: 978-1-4269-9745-7 (e)

Trafford rev. 02/05/2012

 www.trafford.com

North America & international
toll-free: 1 888 232 4444 (USA & Canada)
phone: 250 383 6864 ♦ fax: 812 355 4082

It is my wish to dedicate this book to:

Robbie (Robert) R. Johnson   1958-1991

Brenda S. Hagedorn-Haugaard   1964-2009

Josie L. Harrold   1963-2011

You are loved & missed more than words can express. You have left your traces upon my soul & within my life more than you can know.

A heartfelt gratitude is given to those I hold dear.
I am truly thankful for family & friends both far & near . . .

Thank you, Mom & Dad, for your love & guidance throughout the years. And my sisters, who have helped me to grow through experiences, only sisters can share.

Jeremy & Leihla, thank you for teaching me that a Mother's love knows no boundaries. I am forever grateful for you and with you; I have been able to learn to live life as an adult while looking at all through the eyes of a child. And my beautiful granddaughter, Tyler, you are truly my joy. I am blessed to have 3 of Gods' creatures, 2 dogs & a cat who continually show me unconditional love, while sharing my home with me. The 6 of you are good for my soul!

And last but not least, thank you to my greatest support system throughout this project. Amanda Winter, Brenda Nuttlemann, Jeff Hennesey, Joel Haugaard & Rozann Nelson. Thank you all, for helping to keep this dream of mine alive, giving me a gentle or maybe not so gentle nudge when I needed it. And for reminding me that Faith makes things possible. This book would not have been completed without each of you in my life . . . .

I love you, One &All!

Foreword

It would seem to me words whispered so softly within are the greatest of comforts in this time & place. They often happen so rapidly, unfortunately, I cannot get them all to paper. I will continue to share this precious gift I have been given; to be done for no other reason, other than love.

Knowing where my heart & soul is at is to know the intent from within myself, as well as the intention behind the words when they are written. If they come across to the one reading as positive or negative that is purely by their own design ~ from within themselves. We each see things, as we are meant to.

Power of Love

Because of my Fathers' Love, my life is filled with such beauty that I am blessed to experience with my heart, mind, body & soul. This is also how I love, heart, mind, body & soul, for after having experienced such a powerful, ultimately pure love, I have realized there is no other way to truly love. The love our Father, GOD, shines in every form of life! All Creation! He or She is alive in, a part of, all life! That is Omnipresence! GOD everywhere! The ultimate gift of Love is unconditional freedom, power, wisdom, knowledge of co-creation with our Father. The comprehension of such Love is Awesome, Awe inspiring! With True Faith in GOD, in Yourself, Everything IS Manifested!

Spirit talk for your Soul

Do you listen to; actually hear that small (still) voice in your head? Whether it is your higher self, your Christ self, your Spirit or an Angel speaking, are you listening? Have you opened yourself up to receive the gifts GOD is sending to you, so you can rejoin HIM & our souls can truly be at peace? We have a plethora of knowledge handed down from Great Masters & receptive souls of the past to guide us to the ultimate future. The divine plan laid out for us to acknowledge & receive for centuries & centuries. Freewill is what brought us to this earthly plane—Freewill is what led to our separation from our Father, the "I AM THAT I AM", Our Divine GOD & CREATOR. Freewill is what will take us back to our heavenly kingdom; freewill is what allows us to experience heaven on earth.

While outside, I had a momentary thought of "What can one being, one person do?" Answer immediately; "You are as the ripples in the cosmic ocean—your thoughts, deeds & words are but a single drop causing continuous ripples."

So like a tear that falls upon the water, one tear, it affects & changes many things, everywhere. One person can do so much & is not even aware of the power that their soul contains. Amazing! I have been feeling much like I did when I was a child & would be outside questioning 'GOD' & Creation, wondering about so many things. The innocence of children is so precious; people would do well to pay more attention to the ways of children.

There is so much magic in this world, we just need to open our eyes, open our hearts to see it, to feel it, to tap into it!

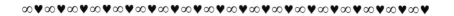

Journey

Take my hand and walk awhile,
Take my hand and make me smile.
With you, I will share my days and nights
With you, we will share Gods' love and light
From my past, into my future you came
Always my present to remain
A love so innocent, a love sincere,
A lifetime of love to forever hold dear.
Take my hand and walk a while.
Take my hand and I will make you smile.

Love transcends all Space & Time!

My wish

Star light, star bright;
First star I see tonight;
I wish I may;
I wish I might;
Have my wish come true this night.
I wish for the love of my lifetime to feel & know the love I hold for him
in my heart & soul. ~ Unconditional love ~

When I look at the moon & stars above;
My thoughts of you are filled with love;
My prayers are sent on wings to God above;
I ask him to bring me the man I love;
My prayers have been answered; I feel it in my heart;
When our life paths come together, we will never part;
For us, two to become one, we are meant to be;
It was written in the stars, our destiny.

Wishes given to the love of my life

May you have your hearts desires come to be;

May you feel the magic of the universe in all you do & see;

May you be blessed with many years of good health & cheer;

May you be surrounded by all that love you & hold you dear;

May you find lifelong happiness & joy in all you seek;

May you be filled with Gods' love & light every minute, hour, day & week.

∞ ♥ ∞ ♥ ∞ ♥ ∞ ♥ ∞ ♥ ∞ ♥ ∞ ♥ ∞ ♥ ∞ ♥ ∞ ♥ ∞ ♥ ∞ ♥ ∞ ♥ ∞ ♥ ∞ ♥ ∞ ♥ ∞ ♥

The love of our Father shines brightly in every soul;

We are so blessed to see that love in everyone we know;

Special blessings of love are shared when two become one;

That love shines so brilliantly, it out shines the sun;

It guides our way to eternal love;

Unconditional to transcend all time, teaching we are all one with our Father above.

∞ ♥ ∞ ♥ ∞ ♥ ∞ ♥ ∞ ♥ ∞ ♥ ∞ ♥ ∞ ♥ ∞ ♥ ∞ ♥ ∞ ♥ ∞ ♥ ∞ ♥ ∞ ♥ ∞ ♥ ∞ ♥ ∞ ♥

Life is full of surprises;

Life is full of joys;

Life is full of love;

All blessings from our Father above.

Life is full of treasures;

Life is full of smiles;

Life is full of grace;

Our Fathers' blessings, traveling through time & space.

Reach for the stars in everything you do;

The magic of love will come shining through;

Guiding you every step of the way;

Gods' Angels are with us every day.

My Gift To You

I give you my heart along with all the love that I hold;
I give you my days & nights as we continue to grow old;
I give you my joy & happiness making every moment treasured;
I give you my honesty for without this, there is no pleasure;
I will share with you my soul & everything it knows;
I will share with you all that I am & will be ~ these to you are my vows.

God is calling to you,
He is beckoning just outside your door.
Trust in Him with all you do.
As everything will work out for the best!
Follow your heart in every area of your life,
It is the voice of God, gently guiding your every step.

As small, seemingly insignificant tears escape from my eyes;

It is in gratitude that my soul needs to cry;

I am blessed beyond measure in this world of Gods' design;

I acknowledge once more things happen for reasons & in His time not mine!

Gratitude for love that fills me & protects me through & through;

A life path I walk holding Gods' hand, His will not mine I pledge to do.

God, my Father, I call to you with love;

Thank you for always surrounding me from above;

My dreams and desires are part of your plan, I pray always that your will be done;

I pray for all of creation to understand, we are all ONE;

Your love and light shine in my every thought, word and deed;

With you in my heart and mind, to fear the darkness there is no need;

I love you Father, with all that I am;

Your truth and wisdom I pour out to every woman, child and man.

∞ ♥ ∞ ♥ ∞ ♥ ∞ ♥ ∞ ♥ ∞ ♥ ∞ ♥ ∞ ♥ ∞ ♥ ∞ ♥ ∞ ♥ ∞ ♥ ∞ ♥ ∞ ♥ ∞ ♥ ∞ ♥ ∞ ♥ ∞ ♥

Hand of God

Hand of God, power and might;
Hand of God, love and light;
Hand of God, holds me forever near;
Hand of God, within it I have no fear;
Hand of God, guards my body, mind and soul;
Hand of God, He is there for all to know;
Hand of God, so grateful for His care;
Hand of God, journey without it, I do not dare!

A beautiful morning star, we call the Sun;
Shines brightly heralding a new day has begun;
Its' brilliant light causing shadows to run;
Enjoy its' splendor, have an adventure & some fun.

The love that is within my heart shines as brightly as the sun;
Giving freely to all of creation as guided by God ~ Loving all as One;
To behold such beauty through the innocence such as that of a child;
Opens new wonders from all surroundings being tame or wild;
Allow Faith, Joy, Peace, Hope & Love from within to continue, spread & grow;
By doing this simple act, the Truth you will behold, the Truth you will know.

It would seem that my words touch the hearts of more than I am aware;
I have been told the words bring happiness & love to those with whom I share;
To touch a heart, to touch a soul;
Is a blessing & privilege to share words given from above to all I know;

Blessings to one & all.

∞ ♥ ∞ ♥ ∞ ♥ ∞ ♥ ∞ ♥ ∞ ♥ ∞ ♥ ∞ ♥ ∞ ♥ ∞ ♥ ∞ ♥ ∞ ♥ ∞ ♥ ∞ ♥ ∞ ♥ ∞ ♥ ∞ ♥

I dream of love, my hearts' desire;
A love so strong, it sets my soul on fire;
Unconditional, tender & caring, it seems I have set my sights;
With wings of love to soar to new heights.

As I sit & contemplate the changes happening day to day;
I hear the words of a friend "let come what may;
My thoughts travel near & far to all I hold dear;
Requesting Angels surround them with love & comfort them, take away their fear.

Life is full of changes; gifts that help us grow;
Bringing with them new adventures & new people that we are blessed to know.

∞ ♥ ∞ ♥ ∞ ♥ ∞ ♥ ∞ ♥ ∞ ♥ ∞ ♥ ∞ ♥ ∞ ♥ ∞ ♥ ∞ ♥ ∞ ♥ ∞ ♥ ∞ ♥ ∞ ♥ ∞ ♥ ∞ ♥

Take a chance; find new joys in this journey called life.

∞ ♥ ∞ ♥ ∞ ♥ ∞ ♥ ∞ ♥ ∞ ♥ ∞ ♥ ∞ ♥ ∞ ♥ ∞ ♥ ∞ ♥ ∞ ♥ ∞ ♥ ∞ ♥ ∞ ♥ ∞ ♥ ∞ ♥

Thank you Father for this beautiful new day;

Thank you for listening to all I pray;

Thank you for holding me in your arms, protecting me with love & truth;

Thank you for allowing your love & light to shine from within;

Thank you for my every thought, word & action;

Thank you for creating & loving me as I am;

I Am Yours.

A blessing to watch a wondrous sunrise this day;

Then magically, mystically another gift came my way;

The river started a new dance of its' own, a mist developing & dancing & reaching as I watch it rise;

Water sparkling, sunlight & magic before my eyes. Take a chance; find new joys in this journey called life.

A prayer to reach my true love sent out with the new sun;

As the star shines, I rise with it searching for the man with whom I will become one;

My heart beats, my soul calls to him anew;

I pray he will be known to me before this day is through.

A journey through life, destination unknown;

With one guarantee, to reap what is sown;

Whether you sing a new song or dance a new dance;

Life will be nothing if you do not take a chance;

Some doors to open, only to have others close;

All part of your destiny, that only God knows;

The magic of Love to come your way;

Blessings surround you each & every day.

As I walk, I look at all around me;

Places, people & things often astound me;

I have always desired to look people in the eye;

For I really have nothing to hide;

I wonder why so many walk with head down;

Watching only the ground;

The eyes they say are the windows of the soul;

Is it fear, shame or just the unknown;

Look at my soul; it is there for all to see;

Just being the creature, I was created to be.

(To love all, not be judgmental, accepting of others, showing a way so others may follow)

So much love I have to give;

A beautiful life I am given to live;

In awe of so many wonders in this place;

Always reminded "Love transcends both time & space";

Searching the eyes, the souls of all who allow;

Knowing someday it will lead to a vow;

Two hearts become one;

Learning together, they outshine the sun;

Nevertheless, that Morning Star will greet them each day;

Always there to show them the way.

One with you, have faith in changes

To completely love those around you is a lesson I had to learn;
By doing this freely, some how it will to you return;
Trusting in a love, an energy within all life;
Makes all worth any pain or strife;
In the end to only give you a new strength;
To live a great life & to achieve all dreams at length.

Dancing with Dragons, flying through the air;
A wonder to see, that nothing can compare;
Magical creatures from a time long past;
Calling to my spirit, knowing I am ready at last.

∞ ♥ ∞ ♥ ∞ ♥ ∞ ♥ ∞ ♥ ∞ ♥ ∞ ♥ ∞ ♥ ∞ ♥ ∞ ♥ ∞ ♥ ∞ ♥ ∞ ♥ ∞ ♥ ∞ ♥ ∞ ♥

Following was written after receiving an email;

Why so much hate?

Why so judgmental towards others because of the color of their skin?
Why can't we see the love that lies within?
Why can't we care & let a healing begin?
Why don't we see that by loving all, it is the only way to win?!

As I awake to a brand new day;
Sunshine from our morning star has come my way;
I look around & what beauty I see;
A multitude of rainbows also surrounding me;
Feeling my heart beat like a drum;
Knowing exactly where all love comes from;
Blue jays & crows sing their precious songs;
A greeting from nature, as the morning dawns.

Like Ripples on the water, my love I send out;

Making a difference, I have no doubt;

These ripples extend through all time & space;

Allowing my spirit to travel to a very special place;

The wonders of creation continually call to me;

Surrounded by Gods' love is the only way I choose to be;

A knowing that all will return from that which I give;

The ripples returning, a life filled with love, I choose to live.

∞ ♥ ∞ ♥ ∞ ♥ ∞ ♥ ∞ ♥ ∞ ♥ ∞ ♥ ∞ ♥ ∞ ♥ ∞ ♥ ∞ ♥ ∞ ♥ ∞ ♥ ∞ ♥ ∞ ♥ ∞ ♥ ∞ ♥

As I look outside on this cool autumn day;

Two Great Blue Herons fly past my way;

A gentle fog rolls in replacing the sun;

Finding a wonderful new day has begun;

So much beauty around everywhere I see;

Praying for all of creation comes naturally to me.

∞ ♥ ∞ ♥ ∞ ♥ ∞ ♥ ∞ ♥ ∞ ♥ ∞ ♥ ∞ ♥ ∞ ♥ ∞ ♥ ∞ ♥ ∞ ♥ ∞ ♥ ∞ ♥ ∞ ♥ ∞ ♥ ∞ ♥

With loving thoughts of those I hold dear;

The love for my children, keeping them near;

Within my heart they will forever remain;

My desire for their lives to be filled with much love & not pain;

With protection, I will ask for them to always be;

In Gods' loving arms blessed for all eternity.

∞ ♥ ∞ ♥ ∞ ♥ ∞ ♥ ∞ ♥ ∞ ♥ ∞ ♥ ∞ ♥ ∞ ♥ ∞ ♥ ∞ ♥ ∞ ♥ ∞ ♥ ∞ ♥ ∞ ♥ ∞ ♥ ∞ ♥

A lust for life if you will;
I cannot seem to get my fill;
Wanting more of everything I see & do;
An adventurous spirit as always, nothing new;
Everything before me clear & bright;
Amazingly, even in the darkness of night.

There is Magic in this Universe, It is called Love.

I awoke before the break of day;
Something calling to me as if someone knew I needed a get-a-way;
So I went to the window & looked around;
Amazed by the beauty I had found;
For there in the gorgeous night sky;
Old friends I gazed upon with my eyes;
A gift I was given before the dawn of our sun;
Surrounded with love from above, my new day begun.

∞ ♥ ∞ ♥ ∞ ♥ ∞ ♥ ∞ ♥ ∞ ♥ ∞ ♥ ∞ ♥ ∞ ♥ ∞ ♥ ∞ ♥ ∞ ♥ ∞ ♥ ∞ ♥ ∞ ♥ ∞ ♥

As I gaze upon my old friends up high;
Looking like brilliant diamonds in nights sky;
Bears, Dragons & Horses that fly;
Women & men that go dancing by;
So in awe of Gods' creation am I;
A blessing of such beauty to behold with my own eyes.

A tall man with beautiful green eyes;
Capable of seeing thru my disguise;
A joy for life he will hold;
Our time together shall never grow old.

A diamond found upon this earth so rare;
Like the feeling of love that fills the air;
A longing to have a life filled with romance;
Never knowing what will be found unless you take a chance;
Grateful for the gift of each new day;
And every blessing I find that comes my way;
The yearnings of my soul found from deep within;
Filled with love & joy for the journey I begin.

∞ ♥ ∞ ♥ ∞ ♥ ∞ ♥ ∞ ♥ ∞ ♥ ∞ ♥ ∞ ♥ ∞ ♥ ∞ ♥ ∞ ♥ ∞ ♥ ∞ ♥ ∞ ♥ ∞ ♥ ∞ ♥ ∞ ♥

Something or someone calls to my soul each day;
"Seek and you shall find, it will come your way;
Search for your treasures," the words within say;
Serenely knowing all will come as it may.

∞ ♥ ∞ ♥ ∞ ♥ ∞ ♥ ∞ ♥ ∞ ♥ ∞ ♥ ∞ ♥ ∞ ♥ ∞ ♥ ∞ ♥ ∞ ♥ ∞ ♥ ∞ ♥ ∞ ♥ ∞ ♥

To have the eyes of love gaze within my own;
Giving a love, so rarely has it been known;
To touch my heart and soul, to make them dance;
Finding it could not happen if not given the chance;
Forever knowing that love has come to me;
Setting my heart and soul on fire, yet setting me free.

∞ ♥ ∞ ♥ ∞ ♥ ∞ ♥ ∞ ♥ ∞ ♥ ∞ ♥ ∞ ♥ ∞ ♥ ∞ ♥ ∞ ♥ ∞ ♥ ∞ ♥ ∞ ♥ ∞ ♥ ∞ ♥

For the changes of this world to begin;
Each must find & understand the love from within;
It is then we can follow the guidance of our heart;
And know we are truly doing our best ~ doing our part;
True love surrounds you inside & out;
Continue your journey in faith casting aside all doubt.

∞ ♥ ∞ ♥ ∞ ♥ ∞ ♥ ∞ ♥ ∞ ♥ ∞ ♥ ∞ ♥ ∞ ♥ ∞ ♥ ∞ ♥ ∞ ♥ ∞ ♥ ∞ ♥ ∞ ♥ ∞ ♥

Some people come into or go out of our lives for no apparent reason;
Much the same as the changing of the season;
Yet others touch our souls for eternity throughout our days;
Loving the traces left upon my heart every moment ~in every way.

Thank you Father for a beautiful new day;
Thank you for the sunshine & happiness that comes my way;
Grateful for a spirit that is filled with a love for life, I hold;
Grateful for the wondrous & innumerable gifts that unfold.

As the mist gently rises from the waters before me;
An unseen friend leaves traces in the ripples I see;
Showing that our presence touches more than we know;
What kind of ripples will you make & where will they go?

What in this world touches your heart?
With what in this world are you willing to part?
What in this world makes you want to sing & dance?
With what in this world are you willing to take a chance?
~The answer for me to all is LOVE~

The reflections on the water, the reflections in my mind;
Take me back to another place, another time;
Some sorrows but much happiness I recall;
And a heart full of love remains through it all.

A Mothers' Prayer

For my children, their dreams & desires to fulfill;
To spread their wings with a full understanding of Freewill;
Making choices & having no regrets as they journey along;
Finding their own voice to sing their own song.

We come to teach & be taught in this life;

To love & be loved in all, happiness & strife;

Having an inner strength is not always looked upon as good;

So often, those you love have their own perception & things are misunderstood;

Acceptance through love for another is the only true gift to give;

Freewill allows us to choose all things we do in this life we live.

Amazed by so many in all they say or do not say to you;

Being judged by another, misunderstood, that is nothing new;

We are taught by all good books ~ "To Love One Another", it IS the One Thing we need to do;

Look within, you will know who you are & that the words ring true.

As the morning frost melts from the tree;

Prisms of light in the droplets I see;

Shown blue, white, purple, yellow & red;

Thoughts of wonder begin to fill my head;

So many gifts we are given;

Surrounded with blessings in this life we are livin'.

∞ ♥ ∞ ♥ ∞ ♥ ∞ ♥ ∞ ♥ ∞ ♥ ∞ ♥ ∞ ♥ ∞ ♥ ∞ ♥ ∞ ♥ ∞ ♥ ∞ ♥ ∞ ♥ ∞ ♥ ∞ ♥

My friend, to express to you before you depart;

A part of you to remain forever in my heart;

So grateful you have been brought into my life a while ago;

To be blessed with a new friendship ~ felt more than you know;

You are a gift to all you touch;

Please remember you are loved so very much!

May you find happiness & joy on your life journey, every step of the way;

Always surrounded with love & protection each & every day.

With my head in the clouds & my feet on the ground;

Calmness, through you Father, from your love I have found;

Awareness of having gifts, that come from within me;

A knowing, the peace, joy & love of my spirit will always be.

The gifts of the spirit come to us from above;

Filling our souls & minds with love;

Sharing of these gifts that are heaven sent;

Knowing we can say ~ A life lived in love is well spent.

Watching the bare trees sway with a few leaves still hanging on;
Listening to an Autumn wind singing sweetly, Winters' song;
Taking nature gently into rest to prepare for Spring to come;
After Summers' warmth I know, I await for glistening snow to blanket the ground I gaze upon.

∞ ♥ ∞ ♥ ∞ ♥ ∞ ♥ ∞ ♥ ∞ ♥ ∞ ♥ ∞ ♥ ∞ ♥ ∞ ♥ ∞ ♥ ∞ ♥ ∞ ♥ ∞ ♥ ∞ ♥ ∞ ♥ ∞ ♥ ∞ ♥

An understanding today, for a while my journey will be alone;
To walk a path in spirit & body to be on my own;
No one beside me;
But GOD continues my guide to be.

∞ ♥ ∞ ♥ ∞ ♥ ∞ ♥ ∞ ♥ ∞ ♥ ∞ ♥ ∞ ♥ ∞ ♥ ∞ ♥ ∞ ♥ ∞ ♥ ∞ ♥ ∞ ♥ ∞ ♥ ∞ ♥ ∞ ♥ ∞ ♥

A friendship held very dear ~ only to continue to grow through the years;
We have shared much laughter, joy & tears;
Always being there in happiness, sadness or fears;
The love we share to remain no matter how far or near;
An inner knowing, any time, any place that for you "I am here";
A friendship held very dear ~ only to continue to grow through the years.

There are those that you love;

Gifts in your life from God above;

Forever through happiness or sadness the love to remain;

A desire to give you all, yet protect you from heartache & pain;

A blessing to see you grow in your life, nothing to stay the same;

Hoping your spirit will always be Free & Untamed;

Watching as you spread your wings each & every day;

Knowing the love held in my heart for you, Nothing can take away.

Waiting for the day, my heart will sing & my soul will dance;

Waiting for the man who will bring love to my life at last;

Ready to give love another chance;

Hoping he finds his way to me fast.

∞ ♥ ∞ ♥ ∞ ♥ ∞ ♥ ∞ ♥ ∞ ♥ ∞ ♥ ∞ ♥ ∞ ♥ ∞ ♥ ∞ ♥ ∞ ♥ ∞ ♥ ∞ ♥ ∞ ♥ ∞ ♥

Sulis my sister, who protects from afar;

Tara my sister, whose name means a star;

Athena my sister, who rules over the moon;

Ma'at my sister, who keeps truth in full bloom;

Isis my sister, who teaches grace & beauty in all ways;

Abundantia my sister, who shares her gifts of plenty in all my days;

Thank you Sisters for loving me, guiding me, teaching me, sharing with me,

our Fathers' ways.

∞ ♥ ∞ ♥ ∞ ♥ ∞ ♥ ∞ ♥ ∞ ♥ ∞ ♥ ∞ ♥ ∞ ♥ ∞ ♥ ∞ ♥ ∞ ♥ ∞ ♥ ∞ ♥ ∞ ♥ ∞ ♥

Love with all your heart in all you do;
Then only, Love can come back to you;
Be truthful with yourself & everyone around you;
Then only, Honesty will surround you!

∞ ♥ ∞ ♥ ∞ ♥ ∞ ♥ ∞ ♥ ∞ ♥ ∞ ♥ ∞ ♥ ∞ ♥ ∞ ♥ ∞ ♥ ∞ ♥ ∞ ♥ ∞ ♥ ∞ ♥ ∞ ♥

Every second, minute, hour, day;
An eternity it feels while I am away;
Every dew drenched morn & every starlit night;
I wish & pray for you with all my might;
So much power in the magic of love;
To fill our hearts with such splendor only comes from above;
A love to share for you & me;
It is our fate, our destiny.

∞ ♥ ∞ ♥ ∞ ♥ ∞ ♥ ∞ ♥ ∞ ♥ ∞ ♥ ∞ ♥ ∞ ♥ ∞ ♥ ∞ ♥ ∞ ♥ ∞ ♥ ∞ ♥ ∞ ♥ ∞ ♥

Moon & stars please hear my plea;
Bring my true love quickly to me;
On wings & a prayer to God above;
Bring my message filled with love;
With my hearts desire I long to be;
Bring him please, swiftly to me.

Being true to your heart—mind—soul;

You can never be led astray—or walk the wrong way;

Being true to your heart—mind—soul;

You can never go wrong with anyone you meet;

Being true to your heart—mind—soul;

You will find completeness in everything you do & know.

I am God's Warrior;

A keeper of His Will;

A fighter of His Truth;

A protector of His Children;

I am God's Warrior;

With Love, I follow His Will;

With Light, I show His Truth;

With Him, I guard His Children;

I am God's Warrior;

His Power is my Strength;

His Love is my Conviction;

HE is my FATHER & I am His Child.

If thoughts become things ~ who stopped the rain?

If every conscious, unconscious & subconscious thought becomes reality, no wonder there is so much chaos in this world—classroom setting for unification.

Becoming ONE, one thought—one action—one with all—one in all—ONE.

Everyone within an area sending out their thoughts, their desires, mixing together, creating <u>what the mixture brings</u>, and then dealing with confusion because it is different from <u>desires</u>. Outcome dependant upon strength of will & combination of like thoughts in each situation.

His love & light;
Are my power & might;
When one goes astray;
I help guide the way;
With Others, Angels & Masters alike;
We come to the aid of one with strife;
To protect a life not yet done;
The others & I, we become one;
To answer a call from our Father above;
I say "yes" & proceed with love.

Sliver

I found a sliver in my finger today, while attempting to pull it out some thoughts occurred to me & have been with me since.

While looking at finger & sliver, trying to see which end was the open end it entered through, I started pushing on the opposite side—at least what I thought was opposite, this was an attempt to verify the opening & hopefully push it back out far enough to get a hold on it to remove it. Mission accomplished, opening discovered, but required more pressure, which caused more pain to get it back out the way it came in. With persistence, I was able to move it enough to grab it & pull it out without much more pain.

Ok, now relating this to our lives! Sometimes we get "slivers" that we are not sure when, where or how they got there. But once we notice them & hopefully long before they become festered, we attempt to remove the irritant from our life. We start looking for the opening it came in through; we start to look for ways to remove it without causing much pain. But sometimes in order to remove this irritation, "sliver", we must go through more pain. With gentleness & persistence, we proceed because we know it must be removed in order to make things better. And finally, we find ourselves back on track, so to speak, irritant gone from our life & hopefully a lot wiser from the experiences we dealt with.

Today on a walk in nature once more;
Brought upon tracks of a deer, my spirit begins to soar;
The beginnings of new adventures have come my way;
My heart pounding gently as if it too, has something to say.

∞ ♥ ∞ ♥ ∞ ♥ ∞ ♥ ∞ ♥ ∞ ♥ ∞ ♥ ∞ ♥ ∞ ♥ ∞ ♥ ∞ ♥ ∞ ♥ ∞ ♥ ∞ ♥ ∞ ♥ ∞ ♥

Some advice, you may take it or leave it, choice is always yours. Pick & choose your battles in life wisely—spend energy worrying about things that can be changed by you—Always knowing you are exactly where you are supposed to be.

Believe in yourself always—you will find an inner strength & knowledge when needed—Having a mind filled with Faith—that things are as they should be; a heart filled with Love & Joy—to be shared; & a voice filled with Laughter—to lift your own spirits higher as well as those around you.

Try to make choices that leave you with No Regrets, Guilt or Shame—Never worrying what others think because they will be right choices for you—Speak from your heart—Try to hold your tongue in anger—Live life to the Fullest & see the Good in Everyone & Everything that surrounds you.
Hugs

∞ ♥ ∞ ♥ ∞ ♥ ∞ ♥ ∞ ♥ ∞ ♥ ∞ ♥ ∞ ♥ ∞ ♥ ∞ ♥ ∞ ♥ ∞ ♥ ∞ ♥ ∞ ♥ ∞ ♥ ∞ ♥

Gazing at the sky in wonder, so grey with patches of blue;

A longing within me to take the steps toward what is before me & new;

Wisdom & knowledge found within pages;

A gift from long ago given through sages;

Truths left untouched through all the ages.

When anger or hate come your way;

Surround it with love in all you do & say;

Given opportunities in life each day;

Choices that are made, always with love I pray;

Changing the outcomes to be the best of life, love to stay;

Believing with heart & soul, whatever is handed out by another comes back their way.

An insight recently revealed;

Due to condemnation by others concealed;

Judgment handed down upon me;

For my true self they cannot see;

I should be known by many names;

It seems association with people & personal practices are to blame.

Alchemist	Muslim
Astrologist	Mystic
Astronomer	Naturalist
Atheist	Pagan
Buddhist	Philosopher
Cabalist	Psychic
Christian	Scientist
Druidic	Shamanist
Gnostic	Spiritualist
Gypsy	Theologian
Initiate	Wiccan
Magician	Writer

And above all, with all, A Child Of GOD

Student—Teacher—Advisor—Confidant—Daughter—Sister—

Mother—Friend—Protector—Provider—Wife—Widow—

Companion—Lover—Traveler—Mechanic——-to name a few more.

∞ ♥ ∞ ♥ ∞ ♥ ∞ ♥ ∞ ♥ ∞ ♥ ∞ ♥ ∞ ♥ ∞ ♥ ∞ ♥ ∞ ♥ ∞ ♥ ∞ ♥ ∞ ♥ ∞ ♥

A man with my name on his heart;
To come into my life, never to part;
A love for each other shared;
To stand the test of time, our hearts spared;
Hand in hand we shall walk;
Truths not lies shall be our talk;
Tall, handsome, a passion for life to see in his eyes;
A love for all & my love returned to me is the surprise!

A love filled life from God above;
A gift sent in truth & love.

Looking for something, someone knocking on a door;
Door is opened not knowing what is in store;
Finding an enjoyment in life with thoughts of asking for more;
Heard, "Ask & it shall be given", so now, I am knocking on the door.

Live life with all of your heart & you can never go wrong!

∞ ♥ ∞ ♥ ∞ ♥ ∞ ♥ ∞ ♥ ∞ ♥ ∞ ♥ ∞ ♥ ∞ ♥ ∞ ♥ ∞ ♥ ∞ ♥ ∞ ♥ ∞ ♥ ∞ ♥ ∞ ♥

Promises given, promises kept;
Promises causing tears to be wept;
To listen to your heart & forget your head;
Living life to the fullest, you will be led;
All in your life when done in love pure & true;
Allowing you to touch so many more than you ever knew;
Promises given, promises kept;
Make only promises causing no tears to be wept!

∞ ♥ ∞ ♥ ∞ ♥ ∞ ♥ ∞ ♥ ∞ ♥ ∞ ♥ ∞ ♥ ∞ ♥ ∞ ♥ ∞ ♥ ∞ ♥ ∞ ♥ ∞ ♥ ∞ ♥ ∞ ♥

I, throughout my life have always been blessed;
Given dreams and visions of the future and the past;
An inner knowing always within me;
My soul or spirit talking about things done or meant to be;
Drawn to people and places in this life now as I am;
Touching my soul through the power of love is Gods' plan;
Even at the times, I have tried to let go of or hide my gift;
It comes shining through again and gives my spirit a lift.

Day to day we journey on, taking nothing for granted along the way;
Following our heart, listening for the words we need to say;
Hopes and dreams are always something to believe in each and every day;
No one told us it was would be an easy road to take but we stay;
To journey on day to day.

My thoughts are of love;
Imagination to become a reality of mine;
Always guidance received from above;
Love to come into my life, the time divine.

My thoughts keep going to one;
Unsure of the reasons why;
It seems my heart & mind comes undone;
So indecisive, intending not to try.

I said again, "I shall bother you No more";
With a mind filled with Faith, Love will shine;
Wondering when & who will knock at the door;
Love brought to me at the perfect time.

To love someone is my hearts desire;
Remembering the magic of thoughts making all real;
Dreams of Love setting two souls on fire;
I know it will be here soon Love to feel.

The man of my dreams will hold me in his arms;
A knight in shining armor will be my King;
He will be made known to me by his charms;
Allowing my mind, my heart & my soul to sing.

My heart reveals, the man of my dreams;
He comes closer to me each day it seems;
My soul, with happiness begins to sing;
For one day, true love God brings;
A future to share, abundance of all things and love;
A blessed gift from God & heaven above.

∞ ♥ ∞ ♥ ∞ ♥ ∞ ♥ ∞ ♥ ∞ ♥ ∞ ♥ ∞ ♥ ∞ ♥ ∞ ♥ ∞ ♥ ∞ ♥ ∞ ♥ ∞ ♥ ∞ ♥ ∞ ♥

The Dragons are calling, my friends from another time long ago;
My imagination gives them new life now I know;
They being majestic, a royalty all their own;
I long to journey with them wondrous places to be shown;
Through time and space they have come to me;
As with all of creation, we are travelers with destiny;
They are beautiful warriors of another time and place;
Yet so full of love, loyalty, truth, mystery and grace.

∞ ♥ ∞ ♥ ∞ ♥ ∞ ♥ ∞ ♥ ∞ ♥ ∞ ♥ ∞ ♥ ∞ ♥ ∞ ♥ ∞ ♥ ∞ ♥ ∞ ♥ ∞ ♥ ∞ ♥ ∞ ♥

So many thoughts through my mind run;
Remembering dreams as a little girl of true love;
Dreams of finding another and becoming one;
While listening to music like "On the wings of a dove".

∞ ♥ ∞ ♥ ∞ ♥ ∞ ♥ ∞ ♥ ∞ ♥ ∞ ♥ ∞ ♥ ∞ ♥ ∞ ♥ ∞ ♥ ∞ ♥ ∞ ♥ ∞ ♥ ∞ ♥ ∞ ♥

Everywhere I look, hearts come my way;

In the bruise on my finger or rocks on the road and the flames of the fire;

I feel as if even nature has something about love to say;

That God knows my heart and someday soon will fulfill my desires.

To Dream . . . Is to allow your hopes & desires to take wing;

To Dream . . . Is to allow our heart & soul to sing;

To Dream . . . For another is to have faith in the goodness to them life can bring;

To Dream . . . Is believing in Something much greater in everything;

To Dream . . . Allows us to soar to new places;

To Dream . . . Brings with it a new reality & new faces;

To Dream . . . We must let our imagination go to new times & spaces.

The Magic of Love brings to my life my Knight in shining armor;

The Man of my dreams for me to Love & Adore;

The One whom I will share a kingdom as a Queen & King;

The Love of God a Magic which all dreams to reality will bring.

Life is a wonder to feel such Love & Sadness within a heart & soul at the same time;

Watching those you hold dear grow in so many ways as they are guided throughout their days;

Praying & hoping the guidance continues to be received & work with the divine;

Thus making their way in this world, achieving dreams & goals along the way.

The gifts we are given are meant to be shared;

To make a difference in the lives of those for whom we care;

Sometimes this means your heart & soul to bare;

Allowing all around you to see Your true self if you dare.

There is a sadness I have found within;

It touches my soul, a new life lesson to begin;

Once it has revealed itself completely to me;

Then a new understanding of my life path I will see.

∞ ♥ ∞ ♥ ∞ ♥ ∞ ♥ ∞ ♥ ∞ ♥ ∞ ♥ ∞ ♥ ∞ ♥ ∞ ♥ ∞ ♥ ∞ ♥ ∞ ♥ ∞ ♥ ∞ ♥ ∞ ♥

Angels whisper gently in our ear;
Loving messages for all to hear;
Listen closely to the love they bring;
You will then with heart & soul begin to sing.

Trust in all that you feel;
Unconditional love makes your senses reel;
Enjoy the blessings in your life;
God gently guides us with grace through strife.

Why does my soul ache so much;
To hear kind words & feel a gentle touch;
A heart filled with so much love;
Only to be alone in the world, like a hand without a glove.

Give with all your heart, not looking for a return;
Then lesson learned will reward you more than you earn;
Give with kindness & generosity in all that you do;
Then only goodness & love will come back to you.

Words come so quickly it seems;
Visions fill my head like dreams;
Love has touched me heart & soul;
Faith has brought me to this place I know;
Wisdom & knowledge a blessing from above;
To share & pass to others, directed in love;
A light of love to brightly shine;
Others to show Eternal love is thine.

One with the Father, One in love;
One with Creation & All above.

∞ ♥ ∞ ♥ ∞ ♥ ∞ ♥ ∞ ♥ ∞ ♥ ∞ ♥ ∞ ♥ ∞ ♥ ∞ ♥ ∞ ♥ ∞ ♥ ∞ ♥ ∞ ♥ ∞ ♥ ∞ ♥

Love returning that once was given;
Freely, completely now I am living;
Fulfilling a destiny, I create;
Knowing for True Love I wait;
Traveling roads known & unknown;
Reaping blessings of all previously sown;
To be touched heart & soul by love;
Soaring to new heights above.

My prayer I send to heaven above;
My wish is to have a heart filled with love;
My true love, a knight in shining armor;
My heart is calling to you whom I adore;
My king to be sharing a love unknown to many;
My love to you given freely & before you, not to any;
My heart beats for you my love;
My soul calls to you my love.

This day my eyes are opened to such beauty & splendor;
I wonder how much of mans' greed can earth endure;
With each beat of my heart, I feel a pain so unmistaken;
The Earth, Moon, & Stars all plagued with a desire to be taken;
Why do so many choose to be blind;
To that which is so easy to see with an open mind;
With an open heart love will only flourish;
This is the only way with true love a soul to nourish;
GOD the ultimate artist of all that is around us;
A living canvas He uses, His thoughts astound us;
Timeless energy creating, becoming one within all;
Patiently waiting for us to hear the call.

As my heart beats within;
I feel the waves of the ocean the twin;
One with all around me;
Sun, Moon & Stars I see;
My soul aches for all to love;
Praying daily all creation sends to GOD unconditional love.

∞ ♥ ∞ ♥ ∞ ♥ ∞ ♥ ∞ ♥ ∞ ♥ ∞ ♥ ∞ ♥ ∞ ♥ ∞ ♥ ∞ ♥ ∞ ♥ ∞ ♥ ∞ ♥ ∞ ♥ ∞ ♥

As I sit & ponder the mysteries of life;

I am given many answers regarding lessons & strife;

A journey to take in love;

The path created while above;

Your destiny is made by the choices you make;

All given freewill a gift for all to take;

Protected by truth in all we do;

The final outcome of your life is entirely up to you.

Today I am told I must write a book;

For the words I share within my heart & soul I look;

A destiny of mine from when time began;

When I said, "Yes, I will help all that I can";

As I put pen to paper and request all to take heed;

To find a oneness with all is our common need;

A love of creation great and small;

Love is the magic of life in one and all.

A Light Within

The light within us, one & all;

Is meant to shine, to heed a call;

We are given this gift of light & love;

Each to shine as bright as the stars above;

One never knows when their light will be the guide;

To help another soul take the next stride;

Love with all your heart in everything you do;

Your dreams and your hearts' desires, your souls' purpose will be set before you;

These gifts also given for you to have and hold dear;

Blessed by the light and love of others that are drawn near.

Thank you Father for everything, for always being with me to help my soul to sing;

As I gaze in the back yard watching the robins dance on snow covered ground;

I find happiness & a smile only nature can bring;

The blue jays, crows & sparrows join in the fun, no cares, no worries just beauty all around.

The Magic of love, the magic of laughter;

Fulfilling a dream and the joy that comes after;

Let go of anger, let go of hate;

Finding the good in all life will change your fate;

Destiny like a web we weave;

What marks on a soul in love will you leave;

The souls in our life, of everything in creation;

Have been drawn to us for lessons & elation;

Whether children, parents, spouses, lovers, pets or creatures in the wild;

To touch & be touched by love as though an innocent child.

I am blessed to be the winner in the sweepstakes of love;

He travels to me guided by angels above;

It is funny, the name of my companion has not been made known;

But the love our souls share long ago had been sown;

We, together as one will journey in light;

All that is abundant & good shall be our delight.

The passions that rage within this body & soul of mine;

Like the waves of the ocean from a soul divine;

To take a walk hand in hand;

Or for a purpose your ground to stand;

The windows to the soul are the eyes it's true;

For when they are clear & bright, the Love shines through.

∞ ♥ ∞ ♥ ∞ ♥ ∞ ♥ ∞ ♥ ∞ ♥ ∞ ♥ ∞ ♥ ∞ ♥ ∞ ♥ ∞ ♥ ∞ ♥ ∞ ♥ ∞ ♥ ∞ ♥

A birthday wish for you from me;

A love filled life & beauty to see;

A heart of laughter & joy yours to be;

Fulfillment of your dreams held by you;

Walking your life path in all that's true;

Under skies above of the perfect hue;

Days filled with light, Nights filled with love;

Shining brightly all around you from heaven above;

Blessings abound & surround you in love.

∞ ♥ ∞ ♥ ∞ ♥ ∞ ♥ ∞ ♥ ∞ ♥ ∞ ♥ ∞ ♥ ∞ ♥ ∞ ♥ ∞ ♥ ∞ ♥ ∞ ♥ ∞ ♥ ∞ ♥

A temptation it seems has come my way;

To keep my true love far from my heart & soul this day;

I ask for protection to keep me from going astray;

My soul longs for my love to find me soon I pray.

My lover, my twin flame, I long for you to be near;

I hear my heart & soul scream out, "Please Bring Him Here";

One day again, I feel I will know your touch;

At that moment realize I have truly missed you and how much!

A lovers gaze to share again & forever known;

A new journey to begin moment to moment unconditional love is sown.

A new beauty I see just outside my window, my eyes partake of a gentle rain & snow;

A soft breeze touching the trees, I wonder which way the leaves will blow;

So calm, so quiet, yet soft whispers from voices I know;

Gentle guidance of love speaking of the path I should go.

∞ ♥ ∞ ♥ ∞ ♥ ∞ ♥ ∞ ♥ ∞ ♥ ∞ ♥ ∞ ♥ ∞ ♥ ∞ ♥ ∞ ♥ ∞ ♥ ∞ ♥ ∞ ♥ ∞ ♥ ∞ ♥

Love, as a ray of sunshine peaking through the trees;
Hugs & kisses gently given by the warm morning breeze;
Nature in its beauty will speak softly to your soul;
A gift given to all, so the creator you may know;
Walk gently with nature it will show you many things unseen;
Many wonders that have always been.

∞ ♥ ∞ ♥ ∞ ♥ ∞ ♥ ∞ ♥ ∞ ♥ ∞ ♥ ∞ ♥ ∞ ♥ ∞ ♥ ∞ ♥ ∞ ♥ ∞ ♥ ∞ ♥ ∞ ♥ ∞ ♥ ∞ ♥

As you walk this path with your heart filled with love;
You find your spirit soaring high up above;
Perhaps on your journey, leaving footprints behind;
For another to follow being of like mind;
Allowing themselves a timeless journey with treasures to find.

I am yours Father to do as you bid. To walk where I need to walk.
To stand where I need to stand. To gently take hold of another's hand.
To speak love filled words, that need to be shared. Showing all around
it is You that truly cares.

∞ ♥ ∞ ♥ ∞ ♥ ∞ ♥ ∞ ♥ ∞ ♥ ∞ ♥ ∞ ♥ ∞ ♥ ∞ ♥ ∞ ♥ ∞ ♥ ∞ ♥ ∞ ♥ ∞ ♥ ∞ ♥ ∞ ♥

I am yours Father, In all that I am.

I am blessed beyond measure;

Given a life full of treasure;

Dealing with mistakes made by man;

God, His Angels, & the Masters all lend a helping hand;

Blessed I am & reminded every moment of everyday;

Faith lives in me & is confirmed by the words I say;

Love continues to grow within me;

Allowing my spirit to guide & defend me;

My path I walk in Gods' loving care;

Knowing my destiny when & where exactly at time I should be there.

∞ ♥ ∞ ♥ ∞ ♥ ∞ ♥ ∞ ♥ ∞ ♥ ∞ ♥ ∞ ♥ ∞ ♥ ∞ ♥ ∞ ♥ ∞ ♥ ∞ ♥ ∞ ♥ ∞ ♥ ∞ ♥ ∞ ♥

Father, in your loving arms I find I long to be;

Surrounded by our Love & Truth always protecting me;

My mind, body & soul are in your Loving care;

Filling me with your Love & Light for with all I am to share

∞ ♥ ∞ ♥ ∞ ♥ ∞ ♥ ∞ ♥ ∞ ♥ ∞ ♥ ∞ ♥ ∞ ♥ ∞ ♥ ∞ ♥ ∞ ♥ ∞ ♥ ∞ ♥ ∞ ♥ ∞ ♥ ∞ ♥

The tears roll slowly down my cheek;

As to God my words I gently speak;

A sadness fills my heart;

From the depths of my soul those tears start;

There seems to be a loneliness to this day belonging;

For those I love, to be near I am longing;

A wish for them to have a life of happiness without pain;

But know full well without sorrows there is no gain;

I am grateful for the Love in this life I know;

Which reminds me to say, "I am not alone—Loneliness go!"

Take a journey today with someone held dear;

Find a place in the mountains by a river or a stream;

You will find new places never before known;

Sit for a while, and to God draw near;

Open your eyes and heart to receive, and then take a chance and begin to dream;

Coming from within you, understanding of yourself you now will be shown.

A call I make to talk with those I hold dear;

To only be turned away for nothing for me is there;

Then as I look through my mail for today;

I find a letter with lots of love has come my way;

Upon opening it I smile at first;

Then, through the dam the tears have burst;

Instant balance I find in so much;

Where some only take, others give with a loving touch.

Seashells, amazingly beautiful with the secrets they hold;

Passed to them from the oceans of old;

Put it to your ear, for its' message it needs to tell;

As messages of ancient wisdom are held within its' shell;

You, like the seashell so beautiful, so rare;

Hold wisdom inside your soul for you to share;

So many will listen far and wide;

You are never alone with God and Angels by your side;

Put aside the doubt, take the first step;

Following your heart, you know your promises are kept.

A walk just taken with a special friend;
A bit different than most, yet the same in the end;
You see, four legs and a fur coat and tail she has;
Bright brown eyes, beautiful and black, with a bit of sass;
I always smile, when time we share;
She gives her love freely, knowing I am always there.

I desire to be held in the arms of a lover;
I desire to share with him, my love and all I have to give;
I desire to have a wonderful man in my life, to start over;
I desire him to be receptive of my heart, a wonderful life to live;
I desire this man to love God as well;
I desire my soul to sing a new song;
I desire for us both our story to tell;
I desire a faith in us to remain forever strong.

Always it seems, I wake with the break of day;

My mind, heart and soul begin to pray;

For all of creation to find a love so true;

Accepting our Father, as we all should do;

Together as one, is the secret to share;

One with God, One with each other, the truth has always been there.

Watching a miracle take place in front of my eyes;

From clouds dark and grey, turning to a beautiful sky;

Along with it, it seems my sadness turns to joy;

The child within me cries out, Oh boy, oh boy, oh boy!

As I stood by the window daydreaming a while;

Words of a greeting came to mind;

A vision I saw, hugging a friend then saying, "It is good to see you again."

The joy in my heart gave my face a smile;

For having a love for another is to always be kind;

At the end of our time together, we will say, "It was good to see you again."

Living a life of love and truth is my choice;

Others around seemingly don't understand the things I do;

But, "that's okay" I hear from my inner voice;

"One day they will accept and understand, then gladly join you";

For on this path I find myself often traveling alone.

Occasionally meeting a kindred spirit who extends a hand;

It seems before I know it again they are gone;

Still feeling their imprint upon my heart, in love and truth I continue to stand.

I have a prayer or a wish if you would;

A man, the one I dream of to come into my life soon;

To receive all the love I have for him alone;

So, patiently, I wait, for my love, as I should;

Knowing one day, our hearts together, we will stare up at the moon;

Having a faith, forever part of my life, never to be gone.

A soul touched with sadness, reason unknown;

A heart touched with love and joy for gifts given and shown;

Words that touch me in so many ways;

Music has touched me deep within my soul all of my days;

Tears stream from my eyes of blue;

A heart that aches thinking of you;

Dreaming of a life, I long to live;

Forever and always, giving of myself, giving all I have to give.

Sitting outside looking about, listening to nature all around me;

Seeing my wildflowers all spent, with their seeds sown for the next bloom;

Hearing the trill of a kingfisher and chatter of a blue jay, then can it be?

My hawk flies over, then a falcon too; as if they knew, I felt a gloom;

A smile to my heart they bring whenever I see them near;

My friends and companions within this life of mine;

Awaiting messages through them from the Angels I hold dear;

Reminding me as with the seasons, changes come in Gods' time.

∞ ♥ ∞ ♥ ∞ ♥ ∞ ♥ ∞ ♥ ∞ ♥ ∞ ♥ ∞ ♥ ∞ ♥ ∞ ♥ ∞ ♥ ∞ ♥ ∞ ♥ ∞ ♥ ∞ ♥ ∞ ♥

Reliving memories of travels made on this earth;

Blessings recalled from my moment birth;

Living this lifetime with the spirit of a gypsy to travel;

In awe of this world, with so much beauty to experience and secrets to unravel.

∞ ♥ ∞ ♥ ∞ ♥ ∞ ♥ ∞ ♥ ∞ ♥ ∞ ♥ ∞ ♥ ∞ ♥ ∞ ♥ ∞ ♥ ∞ ♥ ∞ ♥ ∞ ♥ ∞ ♥ ∞ ♥

Blessed with a son and daughter to bring my life such joy;

I prayed for them both in the days of my youth while talking with a friend;

Dreams becoming my reality because I knew even then, first I would have my boy;

My girl came next, a blessing again, both in my heart 'til the end.

∞ ♥ ∞ ♥ ∞ ♥ ∞ ♥ ∞ ♥ ∞ ♥ ∞ ♥ ∞ ♥ ∞ ♥ ∞ ♥ ∞ ♥ ∞ ♥ ∞ ♥ ∞ ♥ ∞ ♥ ∞ ♥

The knowledge and wisdom we find among pages;
Passed on to all who seek by those who are wise;
Truth and love the way we are taught by sages;
An inner knowing of all that is real upon opening our eyes.

What seems wise to one maybe foolish to another;
Each of us different in what we perceive;
Living a life without harming all others;
Comes back in abundance you receive.

Weave a spell;
Call on the magic of the night;
Desires and secrets to tell;
A handsome man comes to my sight;
In front of a burning fire;
To share each in delight;
Fulfillment of our bodies desires;
By calling on the magic of the night.

With a lover I long to be;
In a short while he will come to me;
Traveling south;
Soon to be, mouth to mouth;
Body to body, before a fire;
Fulfilling the needs of our bodies' desire;
In each others arms;
Experiencing each others' charms;
Indulging our senses;
Having let down our defenses;
With a lover I long to be;
Wondering how much, he longs to be with me . . .

Feeling such a fool;
A new lesson for me;
Taught in this life-school;
I should just let things be;
With age should come wisdom;
Not for me it would seem;
Hoping another would come;
But it was only a fantasy type dream.

Living the life I am meant to live;
Giving all I am meant to give;
Admiring all the gifts that come my way;
I want more, I find I say;
A desire for life has come to stay.

I have removed the blinders, now I see;
All the marvelous wonders that are surrounding me;
Silently I dream, my dreams I set free;
With words gently saying "Believe & so it shall be.

To dream a dream—live life with passion;
To open up to love & know it is returned;
To give all of yourself with no strings attached;
To live life to the fullest with No Regrets.

∞♥∞♥∞♥∞♥∞♥∞♥∞♥∞♥∞♥∞♥∞♥∞♥∞♥∞♥∞♥∞♥

As a new day unfolds,

Bringing many blessings yet untold;

Awake to see the sunrise,

Like magic before my eyes;

A new gratitude for all gifts I receive;

Still hearing the words within my heart . . . Believe & so it shall be,

Believe!

∞ ♥ ∞ ♥ ∞ ♥ ∞ ♥ ∞ ♥ ∞ ♥ ∞ ♥ ∞ ♥ ∞ ♥ ∞ ♥ ∞ ♥ ∞ ♥ ∞ ♥ ∞ ♥ ∞ ♥ ∞ ♥

Just as the river in the right direction will naturally flow;

My life path, I will follow, for it is the right one for me, I know;

Guided by my heart & forgetting my head;

Confident I am where I should be as I am led;

Miracles do happen before my eyes;

Opening my heart to receive a surprise.

∞ ♥ ∞ ♥ ∞ ♥ ∞ ♥ ∞ ♥ ∞ ♥ ∞ ♥ ∞ ♥ ∞ ♥ ∞ ♥ ∞ ♥ ∞ ♥ ∞ ♥ ∞ ♥ ∞ ♥ ∞ ♥

Prayers & love sent to all who lost someone dear;

The love for each other you will always keep near;

A smile will come to your heart;

With every moment remembered that was shared from the start;

The amount of time we are given is unknown on this earth;

But we all leave traces of love from the moment of birth.

∞ ♥ ∞ ♥ ∞ ♥ ∞ ♥ ∞ ♥ ∞ ♥ ∞ ♥ ∞ ♥ ∞ ♥ ∞ ♥ ∞ ♥ ∞ ♥ ∞ ♥ ∞ ♥ ∞ ♥ ∞ ♥

Time is an illusion to be mastered by no one;

Truly measured only by the stars, moon & sun;

Gifts of each moment given one by one;

Lessons learned, dreams become real, live in the now & have some fun.

∞ ♥ ∞ ♥ ∞ ♥ ∞ ♥ ∞ ♥ ∞ ♥ ∞ ♥ ∞ ♥ ∞ ♥ ∞ ♥ ∞ ♥ ∞ ♥ ∞ ♥ ∞ ♥ ∞ ♥ ∞ ♥

My heart & soul call out to the One I love;

Sending my message to Him on wings from heaven above;

A life full of passion we are to live;

Two as One is the love for each other we generously give;

I am knocking at your door, please will you let me in;

Allowing a new journey in our life as one to begin.

∞ ♥ ∞ ♥ ∞ ♥ ∞ ♥ ∞ ♥ ∞ ♥ ∞ ♥ ∞ ♥ ∞ ♥ ∞ ♥ ∞ ♥ ∞ ♥ ∞ ♥ ∞ ♥ ∞ ♥ ∞ ♥

Allowing the love that is within us, that we feel;

To surround all the sorrows in life & let them heal;

Doing this for yourself or others it matters not;

As long as you share the healing power of love that you've got.

∞ ♥ ∞ ♥ ∞ ♥ ∞ ♥ ∞ ♥ ∞ ♥ ∞ ♥ ∞ ♥ ∞ ♥ ∞ ♥ ∞ ♥ ∞ ♥ ∞ ♥ ∞ ♥ ∞ ♥ ∞ ♥

Self respect, the love within;
To love yourself, the place to begin;
First step is always the hardest to take, you see;
From the bonds of fear & the unknown you are free.

∞ ♥ ∞ ♥ ∞ ♥ ∞ ♥ ∞ ♥ ∞ ♥ ∞ ♥ ∞ ♥ ∞ ♥ ∞ ♥ ∞ ♥ ∞ ♥ ∞ ♥ ∞ ♥ ∞ ♥ ∞ ♥ ∞ ♥

The end of the day, exhausted from work;
Wondering why games someone has to play;
Instead of a friend more like a jerk;
Messages come, messages go, how can some be so rude, I'd like to know!

∞ ♥ ∞ ♥ ∞ ♥ ∞ ♥ ∞ ♥ ∞ ♥ ∞ ♥ ∞ ♥ ∞ ♥ ∞ ♥ ∞ ♥ ∞ ♥ ∞ ♥ ∞ ♥ ∞ ♥ ∞ ♥ ∞ ♥

Grateful for all who have touched my heart, my life in some way;
Happy Thanksgiving is the message I wish to say;
May you have an abundance of everything good each day;
Finding & understanding all the Blessings & miracles that come your way.

∞ ♥ ∞ ♥ ∞ ♥ ∞ ♥ ∞ ♥ ∞ ♥ ∞ ♥ ∞ ♥ ∞ ♥ ∞ ♥ ∞ ♥ ∞ ♥ ∞ ♥ ∞ ♥ ∞ ♥ ∞ ♥ ∞ ♥

Forever grateful for all gifts in this life I am given;
Able to hear, see, feel & know the blessings that each contains;
Trying to share with others while in this life I am livin';
As always throughout each moment gratitude for all the love & joy
that remains.

∞ ♥ ∞ ♥ ∞ ♥ ∞ ♥ ∞ ♥ ∞ ♥ ∞ ♥ ∞ ♥ ∞ ♥ ∞ ♥ ∞ ♥ ∞ ♥ ∞ ♥ ∞ ♥ ∞ ♥ ∞ ♥ ∞ ♥

A moment of time can change so much;

By reaching out with a loving touch;

Changing the world around us one soul at a time;

Doing my Father's will—loving all of mankind;

Enjoying the beauty of His creation each day;

Forever know that in love I impact all I do & say.

While out on a walk I see, before me still lay;

Footprints of mine left from another day;

Traces left behind on this earth's floor;

When my heart & head traveled to another door;

Sending thoughts & prayers to the heavens in love;

Knowing now I have also left traces of my heart & soul above.

Yesterday—Thanksgiving, a day to indulge;

Today—my stomach still has a bulge!

My reward was a night of heartburn;

No sleep a reminder of the lesson before I had learned;

Out for a walk hoping more energy to receive;

While my companion, the plan was for her the energy to relieve. ☺

(Ate way too much last couple of days! Why do we make ourselves so miserable while looking for joys?)

When giving of yourself, does it come attached with strings;

Or does the love shine through sharing the blessings it brings;

Choices in living a life of truth or lies;

Truth reveals all where the deception just dies;

Protected by love & truth that surrounds me;

The lies dealt out in this world often astound me.

∞ ♥ ∞ ♥ ∞ ♥ ∞ ♥ ∞ ♥ ∞ ♥ ∞ ♥ ∞ ♥ ∞ ♥ ∞ ♥ ∞ ♥ ∞ ♥ ∞ ♥ ∞ ♥ ∞ ♥ ∞ ♥ ∞ ♥

In darkness & light our paths we travel;

Mysteries of life we try to unravel;

The life we lead whether light or dark;

Is revealed to all as we make our mark;

Heart & soul ~to them both be true;

Your life of love & truth come shining through;

If in darkness it is chosen to remain;

The light will be there waiting to be attained.

∞ ♥ ∞ ♥ ∞ ♥ ∞ ♥ ∞ ♥ ∞ ♥ ∞ ♥ ∞ ♥ ∞ ♥ ∞ ♥ ∞ ♥ ∞ ♥ ∞ ♥ ∞ ♥ ∞ ♥ ∞ ♥ ∞ ♥

Thank You Father for a beautiful new day;

Thank you for all blessings sent my way;

Thank you for taking care of everything everywhere;

Thank you for loving me & accepting my love in return;

Thank you for new ideas, new solutions, new adventures, new love;

Thank you for walking with me on my journey & picking me up when I stumbled;

Thank you for the courage to move forward.

When asked for help, do you turn & run?

Or do you stand as a warrior, staying until the mission is done?

A warrior I see before my eyes;

Armed for battle but in disguise;

A shield of faith & sword of truth held ready to fight;

With the power of love for what is right;

A strength from within so much more than is known;

True colors come to light & to the world are shown.

As sunlight dances on the waters near;

To my heart & soul brings happiness & good cheer;

Remembering how the moon light before has done the same;

And seeing the stars each night recalling their name;

All lights in my life, all there to guide;

Light always surrounds me, never far from my side.

For the songs in my heart I am to share each day;

They are prayers of abundance, truth, happiness & love to come your way;

A light & love I have from within;

Given to all as their days journeys begin;

Take time to see the miracles around you;

Finding each day all are blessings given anew;

As it is given to me & meant to share;

Showing one soul at a time, someone will care.

Madness of Man

The injustices of this world bring a sadness beyond compare;

Making my heart & soul ache as I become more aware;

My Father in Heaven & Angels above;

I call to you for your assistance, in love;

All in this world taking what is wrong & making it right;

Your love & intervention needed both day & night!

~~The depths of my sorrows equal the depths of my love~~

From within my heart a message it calls;

For the earth to sleep, into Winters' slumber it falls;

The river freely moving only yesterday;

Has sunbeams dancing on its' ice as if they play;

A gentle mist rising, reaching for the sun;

An illusion, on the surface stillness has begun;

But underneath, moving freely forever changing & none can see;

The same is also true for you & me.

Some time spent with a friend today;

Touching my heart with words I needed to hear;

Also asked for a swift kick to come my way;

A reminder to stay on the path that has been made very clear. ☺

Watching the snow dance outside;

Staying cozy & warm by the fireside;

While the winter wind blows;

What events this day shall bring, only heaven knows;

Just a glance & so easy to get lost within the snow flying through the air;

For a moment, within myself, I have not a care.

As I awaken to this new day begun;

Being drawn to the warmth of the sun;

My furnace again has decided a pain to be;

Not working as it should, so fireplace still warms me;

Grateful always for the blessings I find;

Forever knowing faithfully All will be made right stays in my mind;

My Father takes good care of me day & night;

To Him, I am always turning even in the smallest plight.

∞ ♥ ∞ ♥ ∞ ♥ ∞ ♥ ∞ ♥ ∞ ♥ ∞ ♥ ∞ ♥ ∞ ♥ ∞ ♥ ∞ ♥ ∞ ♥ ∞ ♥ ∞ ♥ ∞ ♥ ∞ ♥ ∞ ♥

In my minds eye, a panther I see, her coat black as midnight;

With no worries or cares she walks in the light;

She has an inner beauty, is majestic, stealthy & sleek in every way;

Her needs are always met, with courage & strength she stalks her prey;

Always on her intuition she depends for each movement as she makes her way through the jungle in which she lives;

No fear will she show at any moment with any situation that life should give.

A beautiful gift we are given, a gift called life;

A journey we travel surrounded by shadows & light;

There is nothing in this world that cannot be overcome;

If we choose the shadows then comes darkness & strife;

But if the light we follow everything in shadow becomes bright;

When we allow the light within to shine forth in all that is done.

A Gift Given From The Heart

Always knowing the gifts of love, knowledge & wisdom you've given
shall never from me part;
Gifts given freely from the moment of my birth, right from the start;
A parents love, over the years I have come to understand;
With a gentle smile, a hug, & love, always willing to hold your hand;
These gifts you have always given, have helped make me the woman
that I am today;
Teaching me to love more than I think I can, to give all that I have to
give, always knowing more will come my way;
In my heart you will forever be;
You see the gifts you gave will always be with me.

I love you for all you have given & continue to give in so many ways.
Love Always, Rita
(Written for Mom & Dad given as a Christmas gift)

Feeling as though I have stepped back in time;

Me & Mother Nature, a peacefulness that is mine;

As the fire roars & keeps all warm;

The scenery outside has its own mystical charm;

I dare to dream of a future bright;

While daydreaming into the fires light;

One may not realize the blessings that are there;

Until they are made to slow down & feel that love surrounds them everywhere.

As the Phoenix from the ashes will rise;

Mystically & magically it spreads its' wings, soaring in the skies;

Its' tears are said to heal at the time it cries;

I want to believe it is the love within, where its' magic lies;

An immortal creature, showing through death comes life, is no surprise;

And each day we live, we too are gently reminded as the sunsets each days' end, each morn it also will rise!

Believing in miracles such as True love transcends all time & space;
Love strong enough, yet so gentle in each heart, soul & place;
A love felt for another unknown, unconditional & so intense;
An inner knowing it rings truth in every way although it makes no sense;
One day to be held in the arms of love & truth I feel;
Faith within me whispers, "Dreams do become real".

∞ ♥ ∞ ♥ ∞ ♥ ∞ ♥ ∞ ♥ ∞ ♥ ∞ ♥ ∞ ♥ ∞ ♥ ∞ ♥ ∞ ♥ ∞ ♥ ∞ ♥ ∞ ♥ ∞ ♥ ∞ ♥ ∞ ♥

I can feel something calling, pulling me to a mission or a quest;
With some confusion, wondering but accepting it none the less;
Knowing within my heart, as long as I follow it, all will turn out for the best;
A new adventure in my life is about to start while following my heart & forgetting my head;
Reminded that other times throughout my life when I did not listen, I was filled with dread;
Life is not a game of chance, so I walk the path that for me is meant, knowing with Love I am led.

∞ ♥ ∞ ♥ ∞ ♥ ∞ ♥ ∞ ♥ ∞ ♥ ∞ ♥ ∞ ♥ ∞ ♥ ∞ ♥ ∞ ♥ ∞ ♥ ∞ ♥ ∞ ♥ ∞ ♥ ∞ ♥ ∞ ♥

Ever been prompted to do something but left it undone;
Immediately knowing what was chosen was the wrong one;
Living life with no regrets in anything ahead;
Bringing the past into the future, following the heart instead.

Seeing life so differently than most in this world I know;
The mind, heart & soul of each so rare & beautiful to see;
Thinking we are all like diamonds with multiple & unique facets all
our own;
Each adding to the other, as our life experiences guiding us to be as we
should be;
Being open to receiving so many wondrous gifts from all directions as
they are shown;
Each allowed to shine brightly & always grateful I can just be me.

Someone someday loves me & accepts me as I am;
Knowing all there is to know—nothing to hide or hold back;
True Love a gift given, loving all—mind, heart, body, soul, & a gift
received;
To walk the rest of our days, heart to heart, hand in hand.

An adventure is calling to my heart, my soul—a new journey—a new
quest;

Having known the many heartaches in life & blessings at its best;

Reminded to follow my heart to forget my head;

On this path I walk, surrounded by love to a new happiness in life I
am now led.

∞ ♥ ∞ ♥ ∞ ♥ ∞ ♥ ∞ ♥ ∞ ♥ ∞ ♥ ∞ ♥ ∞ ♥ ∞ ♥ ∞ ♥ ∞ ♥ ∞ ♥ ∞ ♥ ∞ ♥ ∞ ♥

Live life with a passion, unleashed from self restraints, follow lifes
adventures to give & receive numerous blessings awaiting like a pot of
gold at the end of a rainbow! ☺

Oh, how I love life & to feel it loving me back!! Blessings

∞ ♥ ∞ ♥ ∞ ♥ ∞ ♥ ∞ ♥ ∞ ♥ ∞ ♥ ∞ ♥ ∞ ♥ ∞ ♥ ∞ ♥ ∞ ♥ ∞ ♥ ∞ ♥ ∞ ♥ ∞ ♥

Looking out the window, there are tracks filled with snow;

Sitting upon the ice, the river frozen just below;

Traces of the journey, left behind to see;

Some side by side, some forming a circle, then coming together again
before me,

Thoughts in my mind—looking outside, "We are all makers of our
own destiny";

Going straight ahead or sidetracking somehow, what kind of path will
be left for another to see.

∞ ♥ ∞ ♥ ∞ ♥ ∞ ♥ ∞ ♥ ∞ ♥ ∞ ♥ ∞ ♥ ∞ ♥ ∞ ♥ ∞ ♥ ∞ ♥ ∞ ♥ ∞ ♥ ∞ ♥ ∞ ♥

With a song in my heart & a skip in my step;
My love for this life has found a new depth;
So much beauty at every turn, breathe taking it in every way;
Yearning within, a mind filled with faith, heart filled with love & joy
& a voice filled with laughter—forever to stay.

∞ ♥ ∞ ♥ ∞ ♥ ∞ ♥ ∞ ♥ ∞ ♥ ∞ ♥ ∞ ♥ ∞ ♥ ∞ ♥ ∞ ♥ ∞ ♥ ∞ ♥ ∞ ♥ ∞ ♥ ∞ ♥

Happiness felt today that has not been felt for a very long time;
Laughter shared with a man from my past, a man when younger used
to be mine;
It felt so right then & began to feel right now as if we had kept a strong
connection;
Then out of the blue, not sure if it was something I said but everything
stopped as if a rejection;
Felt so deeply in both areas, acceptance & rejection, my heart went
from being joyous to an emptiness I would not wish on anyone;
Will somebody, someday just take me as I am—all of me & accept the
love I have to give, someone to love like crazy & who will love me back
the same—a fiery passion as one.

∞ ♥ ∞ ♥ ∞ ♥ ∞ ♥ ∞ ♥ ∞ ♥ ∞ ♥ ∞ ♥ ∞ ♥ ∞ ♥ ∞ ♥ ∞ ♥ ∞ ♥ ∞ ♥ ∞ ♥ ∞ ♥

Life lived with a faith that all will be as it should;
Believe & it shall be the words still ringing in my head;
Dreaming so many things for me & this world would not change that
even if I could;
Understanding they are the dreams of my soul & to my heart they are said.

∞ ♥ ∞ ♥ ∞ ♥ ∞ ♥ ∞ ♥ ∞ ♥ ∞ ♥ ∞ ♥ ∞ ♥ ∞ ♥ ∞ ♥ ∞ ♥ ∞ ♥ ∞ ♥ ∞ ♥ ∞ ♥

A gentle new snow falls just now;

Each snowflake unique, no two are the same some how;

As blessings they fall to the earth this new day;

A calling within me, to make snow angels & go out to play;

Finding such beauty that is before my eyes;

Take a good look around—there may be a surprise. ☺

∞ ♥ ∞ ♥ ∞ ♥ ∞ ♥ ∞ ♥ ∞ ♥ ∞ ♥ ∞ ♥ ∞ ♥ ∞ ♥ ∞ ♥ ∞ ♥ ∞ ♥ ∞ ♥ ∞ ♥ ∞ ♥

Though there are many mountains & valleys in which I walk;

My most treasured journeys are those that with my soul I talk;

Fears of this world I find courage to face;

As many touch my heart in their own way, place to place;

A grace & beauty around me I see;

Strength found within to take the next step on the path before me.

∞ ♥ ∞ ♥ ∞ ♥ ∞ ♥ ∞ ♥ ∞ ♥ ∞ ♥ ∞ ♥ ∞ ♥ ∞ ♥ ∞ ♥ ∞ ♥ ∞ ♥ ∞ ♥ ∞ ♥ ∞ ♥

Remained up late into the night;

Yet called to open my eyes to the day's new light;

My hopes & dreams on new wings take flight;

To the heavens above as an eagle soars to a new height;

These from my heart are to be real;

With me day & night so intensely I feel;

Mind, heart, body & soul all as one;

Gifts received & given allowing all of me to smile as the day is done.

Take a good look at the world around you, what do you see?

So many blessings are waiting for you and me.

When looking at another, do you see the light that shines?

Or is it a bit of sorrow that somehow makes us blind.

Would you take a moment to share a smile, perhaps brighten their day?

A few kind words, sending some love, a small blessing has come their way.

A traveler in my mind, the places I go, my own;

Freeing my spirit for adventure, walking off into the unknown;

An understanding of me, knowing exactly who I am;

Accepting of all others, all part of Gods' plan.

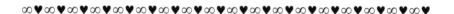

Touching the life of another in some small way;

A smile, a few kind words or just listening to what they have to say.

A companion in my life, moments that we share;

Love and laughter fill the air;

A gentle look or a playful touch;

Making me smile, being loved so much;

Grateful she came into my life only 4 years ago;

For without her now, some of this joy I would never know;

People say in the dog, the master they see;

Must say this is true, sometimes I look at Jaz and see traits belonging to me.

∞ ♥ ∞ ♥ ∞ ♥ ∞ ♥ ∞ ♥ ∞ ♥ ∞ ♥ ∞ ♥ ∞ ♥ ∞ ♥ ∞ ♥ ∞ ♥ ∞ ♥ ∞ ♥ ∞ ♥ ∞ ♥ ∞ ♥

As my heart sings a song, my body gently sways;

To the music of my soul, with a new rhythm it now plays;

"Say what you need to say" and "No regrets", also "Relax! You are exactly where you should be";

All messages, touching me somehow, opening me up, setting me free;

Taking a chance, opening a new door;

I glance around wondering what life holds in store;

In anticipation, I wait to see;

The wonders this life is bringing to me.

Drinking in the warmth of the sun;

Laying in the sand;

Listening to the waves roll in, my heart and its' rhythm become one;

A gentle touch, tracing my skin from a beautiful man, with his hand;

The tenderness within his heart and soul, I see in his eyes;

I give myself completely to him, nothing held back from me;

Understanding everything within each other, through love there is no disguise;

A oneness to be shared by two, all is as it should be.

Giving all that I am, all that I have to give;

Life filled with love, live the life I am meant to live;

Walk with me; talk with me, sharing all we have to share;

Whether for a moment, a year or a lifetime, always knowing the depth that I care;

Make a difference day to day, with a kind word or a smile;

Knowing the love within continues to grow all the while.

My heart to you I will give;

To walk side by side in the life we live;

Love so intense, its' truth we will always know;

Two to become one, on a new journey we willingly go.

Be yourself in all that you do;

For there is no other in this world exactly like you;

Allowing all to see the light of love that shines in every part of your life as you live;

So much, you share of who you truly are in all that you give.

∞ ♥ ∞ ♥ ∞ ♥ ∞ ♥ ∞ ♥ ∞ ♥ ∞ ♥ ∞ ♥ ∞ ♥ ∞ ♥ ∞ ♥ ∞ ♥ ∞ ♥ ∞ ♥ ∞ ♥ ∞ ♥ ∞ ♥

Treasures are revealed to each at the perfect time;

Dare to be open to them, see how they shine!

Understanding them for what they truly are;

Just maybe, it's the answer to a wish made on a shooting star . . .

So many gifts and blessings, not long ago revealed;

By bringing forth a part of my past, within my heart it had been sealed;

Still dreaming of a future, that someday I know will be mine somehow;

A journey I took on that day, in the past, in the future while staying in the present I know now;

Having a fear come over me for my guard I let down that day;

Understanding now completely, being open was the only way.

As I take time for me on this chilly December day;

Watching blue jays and crows, understanding their message they have to say;

Heaven and earth are as one;

Watch and listen for the signs before this day is done.

Magic is in the air, a gift to you is given.

Feeling the beat of my heart, honoring the needs of my soul, understanding the depth of my mind, no greater gift have I known; Walking through life seemingly alone, but that's not a possibility for I am surrounded by a love that is continually there, it keeps up with every stride;
So many blessings my eyes, heart and soul do see, this world it always takes good care of me, as I have allowed for such things to be shown; As my past, present and future have become one, a love for all life held within my heart and there will forever reside;
To live this life without regret, making decisions that cause no heartache or shame, to only give that which I wish to receive, in all I think, say or do, Everything comes back to me, this to well I know.

A time of rest and mystery has found me once again;
Taking time to replenish all of me, all part of the plan;
My cup runneth over, filled with love;
To be shared with others as guided from above.

∞ ♥ ∞ ♥ ∞ ♥ ∞ ♥ ∞ ♥ ∞ ♥ ∞ ♥ ∞ ♥ ∞ ♥ ∞ ♥ ∞ ♥ ∞ ♥ ∞ ♥ ∞ ♥ ∞ ♥

My heartfelt greetings I now send;
To all of my loved ones, family and friends;
Asking for you a life filled with abundance and good cheer;
More than enough to last the coming year;
Happiness in this holiday season, remain safe and still have a ball!
With my heart filled with love for one and all.

My mind drifts away to thoughts of another day;
As I was blessed to travel to the past;
Within my memories brought forward, my heart was cast;
The man with whom I spoke unknowingly guided me there;
As they were of a time we both did share;
To the present a flood of emotions did come;
From a time before when he and I were one;
There the journey did not end for a place in the future some happiness
I did find;
Amazing are the travels when you are one in heart, soul and mind.

A request to the heavens above;
Made from this earth, guided by love;
For I seek the man who honors the needs of my soul;
My prayer is to have revealed his name, so him I may know;
Then bringing together he and I, as one;
To begin a new song as our journey is begun;
A traveler is he, making his way here;
My heart feels him stronger as he draws near;
Beautiful music our bodies, hearts, minds and souls together make;
Having no fear of the chance this time we take.

A peace within, a calmness found;
As I see new snow falls on the ground;
Seems easy to get mesmerized, watching them gently cover the earth;
A blanket so white and pure outside, but in my thoughts it gives new birth;
It lets my mind be wild and free;
Taking me to places I long to be;
With a love in my heart, I go on a journey now;
Believing I will find exactly what I need somehow.

As I sit and prayers come pouring out;

Feelings of my heart, I have no doubt;

Grateful for the love I have within;

A new day starts and a new journey I begin;

Sending all the love and goodness, I can find;

To all of life, directed by my mind;

Finding a fearlessness in giving all I can give;

Opening up to so much, becoming vulnerable in the life I live;

Taking each step with Faith, each and every one that is before me;

Knowing all is well and exactly as it should be.

New snow drifting down, so gently this day;

A voice within I hear, "come out, have some fun and play."

While standing outside tonight for a time;
The voice in my head started a rhyme;
Calls of the night I began to hear;
Two owls seemingly talking came to my ear;
One to the south calling three times first;
One to the north then followed in verse;
They chatted back and forth for quite a while;
A third to the west joined in and it made me smile.
The calls of Mother Nature long into the night;
With a love in my heart, I felt my mind take flight;
There is so much in this life to enjoy and explore;
I have only one problem, my spirit desires more.

Have you ever found an emptiness within you cannot explain?
Knowing its' importance, due to the depth of a heartfelt pain;
Feeling or thinking you are doing everything right;
Giving up something held dear and filled with light;
Life should not be an emptiness inside;
Life should not be filled with a need for something to hide;
To live a life of no heartache and pain;
Means living a life of love unrestrained.

I long to be in nature, the trees, birds and animals around me now;

A place where I can find a peace and comfort some how;

During the day to see the hawks and eagles soaring high;

With night the calls of owls or coyotes come from nearby;

Listening to the songs of my heart and soul, knowing they are mine;

It is easy to get lost for a while, to lose track of time.

A restlessness within my heart I have felt often today;

Needing to express my thoughts, as I know no other way;

To find a way to explain the "crazy" things I do;

I inevitably in my mind, find my thoughts have traveled back to you;

Listening to the words in a song that touches me in a special way;

It is funny; I can hear your voice sing these words in the song I play;

My desires in this life, keeping my dreams alive;

Making my dreams a reality is the goal toward which I strive;

A simple life I choose to live with love in my heart, mind and soul all of my days;

Faith, love, joy and laughter, each with me stays.

On a full moon night walking hand in hand;

As the oceans' waves gently kiss our feet—barefoot in the sand;

Through a lovers gaze I look at you, under the moon and stars above;

Heaven on earth to have you near, filled with so much love;

Being with the man who honors the needs of my soul, always my hearts desire;

Unleashing the passions in each other, in the life together we live, setting our hearts on fire;

A romantic I will forever be;

Grateful for the love you share with me.

I wake early yet within the stillness of the night;

Sitting up in my bed with a stretch and a yawn;

Gazing out my windows, awaiting the mornings light;

Noticing the changes in color from a blue to white upon the snow along with the dawn;

Perceptions of my mind, heart and soul, a part of me;

With the change of each season, a new beginning and an end with each one;

Seeing these changes happen so subtly;

Winter is now here, a time of new beauty and inner reflection has come.

As I sit upon my bed I begin to ponder many things;

Wondering along with the dawn what this new day brings;

Many thoughts run rampant in my mind fed by my heart and soul;

As always, it seems truly the only way I know;

A tear escapes my eyes as one thought occurs to me;

Is there truly a man in this world who can accept all of me for me;

Understanding me and everything I am, everything I do and my beliefs held within, allowing me to share all I have and all I will be;

Capable of loving me, believing in love and truth and seeing all there is to see.

Looking back over the years of my life I have been shown;

In times of happiness or sadness, joys or peace, unconditional love around me, always this I have known;

There is power in prayer, thoughts and the spoken or written word;

Know also the intention behind these, throughout heaven is heard;

So, be mindful yet bold with the words that are sent to others or heavens way;

Try to always surround with love, the things you think, do or say.

Awakened before the break of day once again;

I find myself picking up paper and pen;

Speaking with my Father as morning especially I do;

These words in return come shining through;

"Come to me child, give me all of your cares and worries in life";

"I will take all you have to give, love, fear, and requests for others for their pains and strife";

"Come walk with me child, take my hand";

"I will share with you part of my plan, know that I live in the hearts of all man";

"Come to me child, I will hold you in my arms and show you I care";

"Come talk with me child, receive all I am and have for you to share";

"A life without me, is a life without love; take my hand; I will be with you all your days;"

"Send to me all that is within you, your love, dreams, desires of life, your fears and worries, to the heavens let them be raised";

"Take my hand, do not be afraid";

"For always around you, my love, light and protection have been laid".

My mind, my heart brings forth the words I say;

To my Father above and the Angels too;

I ask, all to be filled with love each and every day;

That all is protected and are open to hear the guidance given to you;

May you all find Blessings, Abundance in all that is good, and Be safe in your travels I pray.

Trusting that all needs are taken care of in all my days and nights;

Discovering life's beauty in every moment I am;

Understanding so much more, being open to love and light;

Believe and it shall be—all part of Gods' divine plan.

Amazed by the intensity of all that I feel;

In awe of my dreams that are today real;

Knowing there is so much more . . . more than I can comprehend;

A life of joy, compassion, love, a passion like a fire that burns within . . . mine to the end . . . .

∞♥∞♥∞♥∞♥∞♥∞♥∞♥∞♥∞♥∞♥∞♥∞♥∞♥∞♥∞♥∞♥

Ever sat, closed your eyes and let yourself go?

Ever feel as though you hear things through music, etc. exactly when those things you needed to hear?

Ever wonder if you are where you need to be?

Ever trust in something so much greater than you?

You KNOW that everything happens for a reason,

NO MATER WHAT . . .

My thoughts turn to you, at times I feel weak;

My heart opens up and my voice begins to speak;

Believing with all that I am or ever will be, You are always by my side;

Sending your love and light to be my guide;

Never knowing at the moment the type of messenger you will send or what I will be told;

An Angel to softly whisper or the kind words of a friend just down the road.

As the day goes on, if I find within me a fear;

It is to my Father, whom I speak, drawing Him near;

Sharing with Him, all of my sorrows and cares;

Letting go of my fears and troubles through prayers;

Placing every area of my life completely in His hands;

Trusting everything is part of a divine plan.

Some time ago visiting with a dear friend of mine;

She is wise beyond her years and her soul cannot help but shine;

These words she did say, "When you hear something twice in the same day,

God is talking to you."

The moment she said it, I knew it was true;

As I began having doubt about a project before me;

Unknowingly perhaps, this day two times I heard the words that I needed,

from the doubt I was set free.

Happiness is . . .

In the giving and receiving

In the hoping and believing

In the sharing and caring

In the showing and knowing

In the seeking and finding

Giving all of yourself in all you do;

Receiving openly what is given to you;

Hoping for the best always to be;

Believing in miracles, they are there for us to see;

Sharing of your love and all that you feel;

Caring for those who are dear, with compassion, it just may be a heart you help heal;

Showing who you truly are in every area as you live;

Knowing in truth, we get what we give;

Seeking all of your dreams and desires in this life, as each day goes by;

Finding them near and far, treasures for you, but only if you try.

Blessings abound through a miracle of birth;

In all life here on earth;

With the Angels in heaven and the stars there too;

Messengers given of old for me and you;

God the Creator, maker of all that ever was, is or shall be;

A Father giving His Greatest Gift—Love—always to you and me.

Thank you Father for your Love and Light;

That shines within me and continues to burn bright.

To escape this world, I go into my mind;

For there, peace and contentment I can find;

Bringing forth dreams that are truly mine;

Upon closing my eyes, the visions become real;

To another time and place perhaps, there is so much to feel;

Allowing for a time my heart and soul to heal.

God is the keeper of the key;

That shall unlock the door that stands before me;

As one door closes in life, to another I am led to open;

Behind it is new wisdom and adventures, the ones for which I am hoping;

Going forward I must, take a new chance;

Finding new gifts, new songs and possibly a new dance.

Last night while outside I got to again see the moon;

Behind the clouds and it's gone, I long to see it again soon;

This day as I rise, a blessing to see the sun;

Normal everyday simplicities to have and take for granted, as each day is ended or begun.

Earlier today a special gift, I did receive;

A phrase repeated over and over in my head—the words, I believe;

"Something that is missing is coming back to you";

I sobbed when I realized that the words are true.

As the morning sun rises, chasing away the shadows of the night;

I behold such beauty, like that of diamonds in the snow, a wondrous delight;

The frost on the trees glistening, as it is kissed by the sun;

As a new day dawns again, this place, my heart has won.

There is so much to be said with seemingly so little time to say it;

Each and every day as my world around me starts, with my Father I sit and visit;

My prayers and requests, I have learned to express;

I give Him my loves, desires, worries and fears; He in turn gives me rest.

On this day, so bright and sunny;

Truths revealed to my heart;

Treasures to hold forever.

Simple things in life bringing a smile to my face;
Hearing a child's' laughter or watching a snowflake drifting down with such grace;
Reaching out to someone sharing tears or joys for a time if you will;
Making new memories, finding happiness and love for your heart to fill.

∞ ♥ ∞ ♥ ∞ ♥ ∞ ♥ ∞ ♥ ∞ ♥ ∞ ♥ ∞ ♥ ∞ ♥ ∞ ♥ ∞ ♥ ∞ ♥ ∞ ♥ ∞ ♥ ∞ ♥

What dreams or desires are held within your heart, your soul?
What wishes or hopes do you have that would make you complete, make you whole?
With open eyes, an open mind and an open heart, I live each day new;
With a strong love and faith I believe, "something that is missing, is coming back to you", words given that ring true;
Have you ever searched for answers and found they have always been within you?

∞ ♥ ∞ ♥ ∞ ♥ ∞ ♥ ∞ ♥ ∞ ♥ ∞ ♥ ∞ ♥ ∞ ♥ ∞ ♥ ∞ ♥ ∞ ♥ ∞ ♥ ∞ ♥ ∞ ♥

As I send a message recently;
I get distinct feelings, "to just let them be";
So much, at times, I get confused;
So many others, I must amuse;
My heart feels an emptiness I can't explain;
Sometimes I wonder, if alone I am to remain.

∞ ♥ ∞ ♥ ∞ ♥ ∞ ♥ ∞ ♥ ∞ ♥ ∞ ♥ ∞ ♥ ∞ ♥ ∞ ♥ ∞ ♥ ∞ ♥ ∞ ♥ ∞ ♥ ∞ ♥

As we travel our path, a willing journey to somewhere;
We experience much: some love, some sorrow, some pain, causing
wounds and scars;
If we allow, it will teach us to give more and for others to care;
Then on this journey in life, we can truly share who we are.

Have you ever believed in something so much, it felt like it came from
the depths of your soul?
Anticipating its' arrival, yet the longer it takes the more your heart
aches, feeling like your not whole;
Have you ever felt as though perhaps you were lucky enough and life
gave you a second chance for happiness?
Take a risk, if you do not you will never know, if love was outside your
door, waiting for you to say "yes".

While I sat and stared at the trees a while;

Upon my face appeared a smile;

Realizing there is so much in front of us we do not see;

Because after some time of looking at the same place, I saw a deer eating before me;

As I still watch it, no cares or worries does it show;

Gently rummaging, it takes all the time it needs, it is safe and cared for it seemingly knows;

A gentle reminder to open my eyes and my heart to see;

All will be made clear, because it is right in front of me.

A kiss from the mornings' sun;

Sent to a traveler as this day is begun;

For a journey blessed beyond compare;

There is happiness, joy and peace in the air;

I love to gaze upon our morning star;

Knowing it is with you, wherever you are.

A peace within has come my way;
Like a balance of self is here to stay;
A troubled mind and troubled heart no more;
Love has chased those fears from my door.

Life will always have its' twists and turns;
With lessons in each, for all involved to learn;
One day unknown, an old friend may come back to stay;
Or a newer friend may turn and walk away;
As one door is closed, leaving some things or people behind;
Another can be opened, I pray what you are seeking you find.

Well now, last day of the year, 2009 is here at last;

What once was our future is now part of our past;

Upon reflecting over this last year;

I am reminded of so much Love, Happiness, Joys, some Sadness and even some Fear;

The cycle of life is an amazing thing;

With all endings come new beginnings, in everything.

Having realized so many dreams and facing so many fears;

It is hard not to see all of the blessings received over this past year;

Watching those held dear, spread their wings and soar to new heights;

Perhaps with a touch of sadness, but knowing the outcome brings delight;

Remembering always, we get what we ask for, in love it is given to us;

Upon its reception, acceptance of our requests is a must;

Trusting in the love and light that surrounds us day and night;

Taking the blinders off—the world, life that is around us is a beautiful sight.

When mind, body and soul, the three become one;
With the rhythm of the heart beating like a drum;
A divine love and light come shining through;
There for all to see in all that you think, say or do;
Whether saying a prayer for someone dear;
Or all of creation, far or near;
That simple thought, gesture if you will;
Making a difference for others, yet your destiny you fulfill.

Creators of our life, we are all given the ability to be;
Capable of creating such beauty for all the world to see;
Some are musicians, writing music and lyrics to their lifes' song;
Also given a voice of beauty to sing along;
Some are artists, painting their lifes' portrait with every stroke of the brush;
Colors of such magnitude taking ones' breath away while gazing upon the canvas into their world you are thrust;
Some are weavers using brilliantly colored threads in their beautiful tapestry;
Showing in richness, love, joy, sadness or pain, moments within their life path,
their destiny;
Some are writers, expressing their life with paper and pen;
Creating a view to share with a friend;
No matter how we create, it is not necessarily one of the examples above;
But creators we all are, so be a creator through love!

A wish upon a star earlier I did make;

Sending a prayer to heaven with wings it to take;

Afraid to look at the phone, feeling disappointment I will find;

Yet a knowing I've been given, an answer within my heart, within my mind;

Have you ever had an idea, something you believe in so much it just has to be true;

Believing in a dream with all your mind, all your heart, with an understanding it will be real, it will find a way to you, I do!

Good morning Father—I thank you for this special day;

For all of the beauty you send my way;

"There are many 'special days' in front of you";

"Believe in yourself and know it is true";

As I feel the beat of my own heart, Father I trust in you.

Today has been a wonderful day in every way;
These feelings I feel, I long for them to stay;
I think of you and my heart begins to race;
I close my eyes and my mind sees your face;
Some how I know time will slow for a while;
And when you are here, it will speed up and my heart will smile.

Who is it that is always there when I fall;
Who is it I turn to, who do I call;
My Father, and the Angels as well as Masters who have walked this
earth before;
They are all there, waiting, I must only knock on the door;
Always there again and again to help me stand;
Listening closely, they say, "Here Child, Here I am."

I give you my heart, two becoming one, together one rhythm they make;
I give you my heart, and all the love within that it holds, it waits for
you to take;
I give you my love, together as one, together we grow old;
I give you my love felt from the depths of my soul forever I am yours
to have and to hold.

Knowing things I know, feeling all that I feel;

The depth of it all makes my mind reel;

In submission to another, I willingly give all;

Seeing for the first time it is given back in a measure truly equal;

Trusting in this one, with my mind, body, heart and soul;

With everything I am, with everything I know.

So many gifts I receive in numerous ways;

Love touching my heart, my soul, lasting all of my days;

Having realized completely, I am still in the care of the Potters' hands;

A few days ago I literally dropped to my knees—and He is who again helped me to stand;

This day I received a picture of just that, me being submissive to my Father,

whom I trust;

Seeing His blessings, His love, in everything, believing I am supposed to be and continue on my journey as I must.

∞ ♥ ∞ ♥ ∞ ♥ ∞ ♥ ∞ ♥ ∞ ♥ ∞ ♥ ∞ ♥ ∞ ♥ ∞ ♥ ∞ ♥ ∞ ♥ ∞ ♥ ∞ ♥ ∞ ♥ ∞ ♥

Gifts I received late into the night;

Revealing so much, shining so bright;

From the prisms from my crystal cast by the light of the moon;

Reminding me, my love is to be with me very soon;

A picture, a message in the form of a text;

Reminding me God is still with me, always leading me to what comes next;

Then in my dreams I visit the man whom brings my heart delight;

Traveling to his side during a clear starlit night;

To be awakened in the morning with the light of the sun;

More prisms from my crystal just as my day is begun.

When anything done whole heartedly, a selfless act;

With no hidden agenda, no strings attached;

Not knowing how it will be received;

Still taking a chance in following your heart & with faith, believe.

Have you ever loved something or someone so much you could set them free?
To learn & grow, experiencing the life for them that is meant to be;
For in truth they are not a possession to be owned;
If the life is one to be shared to see love freely returned, unconditionally it is known.

To reveal yourself to another, completely, nothing hidden, no strings attached;
Finding an acceptance of all you are and love is given back;
Knowing that another is with you freely by their choice, giving of themselves in the life that is shared;
Then in truth all is known, given unquestionably, showing the depth that we care.

∞ ♥ ∞ ♥ ∞ ♥ ∞ ♥ ∞ ♥ ∞ ♥ ∞ ♥ ∞ ♥ ∞ ♥ ∞ ♥ ∞ ♥ ∞ ♥ ∞ ♥ ∞ ♥ ∞ ♥ ∞ ♥ ∞ ♥

In everything I do & everything I say;
Trying to be careful not to harm another in any way;
Sending my love in my thoughts through prayer throughout the day & night;
Then knowing at the end of my day, I can rest knowing I have done what is right.

∞ ♥ ∞ ♥ ∞ ♥ ∞ ♥ ∞ ♥ ∞ ♥ ∞ ♥ ∞ ♥ ∞ ♥ ∞ ♥ ∞ ♥ ∞ ♥ ∞ ♥ ∞ ♥ ∞ ♥ ∞ ♥ ∞ ♥

I am the creator of my own happiness, sorrows or fears;

I am the only one who can allow the shedding of tears;

I am the one who has the power to feel what I feel;

I am the source behind making my dreams very real.

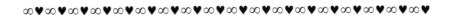

Knowing there is much power within all in creation;

Understanding thoughts, words & actions are what gives life to the fears, sorrows or elation;

We get what we give, it is the universal law;

Seeing that we get what we ask for, for ourselves or for others—I am in Awe.

∞ ♥ ∞ ♥ ∞ ♥ ∞ ♥ ∞ ♥ ∞ ♥ ∞ ♥ ∞ ♥ ∞ ♥ ∞ ♥ ∞ ♥ ∞ ♥ ∞ ♥ ∞ ♥ ∞ ♥ ∞ ♥

Treasures from heaven lay upon the ground;

Glistening like diamonds waiting to be found;

Nature in its splendor in my sight as I look around;

Treasures from heaven through love I have found.

∞ ♥ ∞ ♥ ∞ ♥ ∞ ♥ ∞ ♥ ∞ ♥ ∞ ♥ ∞ ♥ ∞ ♥ ∞ ♥ ∞ ♥ ∞ ♥ ∞ ♥ ∞ ♥ ∞ ♥ ∞ ♥

I must be patient to receive a wondrous gift;
A gift I have dreamed of & prayed for, with all my spirit I uplift;
Arriving at the time it is meant to be;
Understanding the essence of perfect harmony;
The love of my lifetime is on his way to me;
Soon to be here, sharing a love to last all eternity.

I am drawn to the new fallen snow;
Illuminated by the sun this morn, I see it shimmer & glow;
Looking like a painters canvas with shadow & light;
A calmness, it fills me as I gaze upon the sight.

∞ ♥ ∞ ♥ ∞ ♥ ∞ ♥ ∞ ♥ ∞ ♥ ∞ ♥ ∞ ♥ ∞ ♥ ∞ ♥ ∞ ♥ ∞ ♥ ∞ ♥ ∞ ♥ ∞ ♥ ∞ ♥

I send forth ripples of love & light;
With every beat of my heart, with all my might.

∞ ♥ ∞ ♥ ∞ ♥ ∞ ♥ ∞ ♥ ∞ ♥ ∞ ♥ ∞ ♥ ∞ ♥ ∞ ♥ ∞ ♥ ∞ ♥ ∞ ♥ ∞ ♥ ∞ ♥ ∞ ♥

I love you Father with all that I am;

I am grateful for all that you do, with every beat of my heart, all of my mind & from the depths of my soul;

I am yours, I am yours, I AM YOURS.

The sun rises this day;

And its' "dogs" has brought out to play;

Also seeing the moon in the morning sky;

As if saying "catch me if you can, I dare you to try";

Blessings all around as this new day is begun;

My spirit wanting to join in the fun.

With calmness, peace—contentment within;

A beautiful new day in my journey I begin;

Many thoughts I ponder & many prayers I send out;

Even knowing the freewill of others can stop the prayers sent to them, through their own doubt;

But there is strength in numbers as we all have been shown;

And with the faith within, great things for the better may be sown.

Such vivid dreams I am given in the night;

With love & laughter & colors so bright;

Conversations & music, natural beauty all around;

Even in my dreams I "Thank GOD" for what he gives me I have found.

∞ ♥ ∞ ♥ ∞ ♥ ∞ ♥ ∞ ♥ ∞ ♥ ∞ ♥ ∞ ♥ ∞ ♥ ∞ ♥ ∞ ♥ ∞ ♥ ∞ ♥ ∞ ♥ ∞ ♥ ∞ ♥ ∞ ♥

As I awaken from a dream of such beauty & splendor;

Surrounded by love & music to my Father I surrender;

For a time, I traveled in another place so real;

Upon waking I bring with me the emotions I did feel;

With joy in my heart, I go forth in this new day;

Knowing wonderful gifts in life are coming my way.

∞ ♥ ∞ ♥ ∞ ♥ ∞ ♥ ∞ ♥ ∞ ♥ ∞ ♥ ∞ ♥ ∞ ♥ ∞ ♥ ∞ ♥ ∞ ♥ ∞ ♥ ∞ ♥ ∞ ♥ ∞ ♥ ∞ ♥

As I lay in bed looking outside, the new day to greet;

4 deer pass by walking south on the frozen river as if it's a snow covered street;

Smiling at this gift, taking it in, 4 more go trotting by;

A 3rd group of 4 then meets my eye;

Blessings abound already on this beautiful new day;

Excited to receive all the gifts heaven & earth are sending my way;

(note: 12 to the south & 1 to the north in about 10 minutes time 4-4-4-)

∞ ♥ ∞ ♥ ∞ ♥ ∞ ♥ ∞ ♥ ∞ ♥ ∞ ♥ ∞ ♥ ∞ ♥ ∞ ♥ ∞ ♥ ∞ ♥ ∞ ♥ ∞ ♥ ∞ ♥ ∞ ♥ ∞ ♥

From a winters' slumber, I awaken from my sleep;
But my dreams, alive in my heart I will keep;
Ah, the winter wonderland that now lays before my eyes;
Pristine, crystal covered trees, such beauty has no disguise.

∞ ♥ ∞ ♥ ∞ ♥ ∞ ♥ ∞ ♥ ∞ ♥ ∞ ♥ ∞ ♥ ∞ ♥ ∞ ♥ ∞ ♥ ∞ ♥ ∞ ♥ ∞ ♥ ∞ ♥ ∞ ♥ ∞ ♥

Amazed by the innumerable gifts we are blessed with each day;
The laughter & smiles, fog within the night or songs the radio does play;
Simple little things that can touch a heart with unconditional love;
Letting the mind & heart sing, the soul dance as they soar to new heights above.

∞ ♥ ∞ ♥ ∞ ♥ ∞ ♥ ∞ ♥ ∞ ♥ ∞ ♥ ∞ ♥ ∞ ♥ ∞ ♥ ∞ ♥ ∞ ♥ ∞ ♥ ∞ ♥ ∞ ♥ ∞ ♥ ∞ ♥

As I sit & listen to the music, the rhythm my heart makes;
My mind sings along joining in, preparing for a journey I am to take;
My soul starts to dance in step with the other two;
Seeing so much with an open mind, an open heart, knowing there is much when they are One, we are able to do.

∞ ♥ ∞ ♥ ∞ ♥ ∞ ♥ ∞ ♥ ∞ ♥ ∞ ♥ ∞ ♥ ∞ ♥ ∞ ♥ ∞ ♥ ∞ ♥ ∞ ♥ ∞ ♥ ∞ ♥ ∞ ♥ ∞ ♥

Perfectly imperfect, is how I describe me;
Ultimately I am made just as I am meant to be.

∞ ♥ ∞ ♥ ∞ ♥ ∞ ♥ ∞ ♥ ∞ ♥ ∞ ♥ ∞ ♥ ∞ ♥ ∞ ♥ ∞ ♥ ∞ ♥ ∞ ♥ ∞ ♥ ∞ ♥ ∞ ♥

Prayers are heaven sent this day as everyday;
For those held dear & those I have not met;
Asking that love, light, insight & healing come their way;
Knowing that all needs are taken care of, even if it is not visible yet.

∞ ♥ ∞ ♥ ∞ ♥ ∞ ♥ ∞ ♥ ∞ ♥ ∞ ♥ ∞ ♥ ∞ ♥ ∞ ♥ ∞ ♥ ∞ ♥ ∞ ♥ ∞ ♥ ∞ ♥ ∞ ♥

Finding happiness in my life, right now;
Not expecting a thing but knowing, accepting all my needs are met
somehow;
Grateful for everything, everyone in my life throughout each day & night;
Having faith, I am on the path, for me, that is right.

∞ ♥ ∞ ♥ ∞ ♥ ∞ ♥ ∞ ♥ ∞ ♥ ∞ ♥ ∞ ♥ ∞ ♥ ∞ ♥ ∞ ♥ ∞ ♥ ∞ ♥ ∞ ♥ ∞ ♥ ∞ ♥

The love I give, the love I share;

The intention behind to show I care;

The life I live, the web I weave;

The maker of my own destiny I truly believe;

The responsibility of my own deeds, words & thoughts;

The accountability for walking the path in this life I have sought.

The love for life, held in the simplest form;

Knowing we are one from the day we are born;

Closer to some than others it would seem to be;

Due to life lessons & joys, all part of our destiny;

Life choices we make, through freewill we decide;

But the Universal Laws, All Must Abide.

Awakened again before the break of day;

Surrounded by fog yet I know I can find my way;

If I begin to feel lost, my intuition will be my guide;

And in Love & Protection, I always have GOD & His Angels by my side.

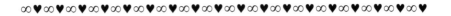

There are Angels among us, near & far;

Some are always with you, no matter where in life you are;

Some are strangers sharing a glance, or maybe stranded & in need of your aid;

Maybe they are here to test who you are or to help a debt to be paid;

Some are your friends, there when you need them & don't know it;

But revealing their hearts & not afraid to show it.

With my heart filled with dreams;

With my mind filled with faith;

With anticipation for life's adventures it seems;

With a new found patience I lovingly wait;

With an inner knowing of wondrous miracles that come my way;

With so much gratitude felt from the depth of my soul;

With giving all I have to give each & every day;

With a love unconditional completing me, making me whole.

∞ ♥ ∞ ♥ ∞ ♥ ∞ ♥ ∞ ♥ ∞ ♥ ∞ ♥ ∞ ♥ ∞ ♥ ∞ ♥ ∞ ♥ ∞ ♥ ∞ ♥ ∞ ♥ ∞ ♥ ∞ ♥

Having found a love so great, it is hard to comprehend;

Having faith in this love, having a beginning & a happily ever after 'til the end.

∞ ♥ ∞ ♥ ∞ ♥ ∞ ♥ ∞ ♥ ∞ ♥ ∞ ♥ ∞ ♥ ∞ ♥ ∞ ♥ ∞ ♥ ∞ ♥ ∞ ♥ ∞ ♥ ∞ ♥ ∞ ♥

A peace & tranquility fills the air;
A stillness settled seemingly everywhere;
No movement on the earth, in the air or on the water;
Only the fire in the sky illuminating the beauty before me.

A dense fog having visited in the night;
Working its magic before the mornings light;
The wonders of this earth always a surprise;
Capable of changing reality right before my eyes.

The peace you seek, I pray you soon find;
An understanding of love & life that can only be thine;
To share the gifts you are given with so many that stand before you;
Believing with all your heart, mind & soul, changing all for the better
with everything you think, say or do.

For every choice in this life freely we make;
For every step in this life freely we take;
For every lesson in this life freely we have chosen to learn;
For every blessing in this life freely we give in return.

∞ ♥ ∞ ♥ ∞ ♥ ∞ ♥ ∞ ♥ ∞ ♥ ∞ ♥ ∞ ♥ ∞ ♥ ∞ ♥ ∞ ♥ ∞ ♥ ∞ ♥ ∞ ♥ ∞ ♥ ∞ ♥

Forever grateful for every moment every day;
Each moment being a blessing sent my way;
Our Fathers Love eternally steadfast & true;
Only requiring from yourself, Faith for the miracles that come to you.

∞ ♥ ∞ ♥ ∞ ♥ ∞ ♥ ∞ ♥ ∞ ♥ ∞ ♥ ∞ ♥ ∞ ♥ ∞ ♥ ∞ ♥ ∞ ♥ ∞ ♥ ∞ ♥ ∞ ♥ ∞ ♥

So many things changing while many stay the same;
So many finding happiness & still many try to place blame;
So many finding peace & love within themselves;
So many living in the past, placing their future up on a shelf;
Having responsibility for my own happiness always;
Knowing I am accountable for my own feelings towards myself &
others all of my days.

∞ ♥ ∞ ♥ ∞ ♥ ∞ ♥ ∞ ♥ ∞ ♥ ∞ ♥ ∞ ♥ ∞ ♥ ∞ ♥ ∞ ♥ ∞ ♥ ∞ ♥ ∞ ♥ ∞ ♥ ∞ ♥

To be awakened in my dream with love from a man;

To be awakened in reality with words from his hand;

To feel his lips on my own & be in his arms within my dream a precious gift;

To be accepted for all I am gives my heart & soul a lift.

A life of new beginnings each day a brand new start;

But with beginnings there are endings, from something we must always part;

Trusting that what was old is being replaced with something better than what we had before;

Knowing you are always surrounded in love taking a chance & walking through that open door.

Thank You Father for this beautiful new day;

Thank You for all the blessings you send my way;

Thank You for always loving me;

Thank You for your guidance helping me to become the woman I am meant to be.

∞ ♥ ∞ ♥ ∞ ♥ ∞ ♥ ∞ ♥ ∞ ♥ ∞ ♥ ∞ ♥ ∞ ♥ ∞ ♥ ∞ ♥ ∞ ♥ ∞ ♥ ∞ ♥ ∞ ♥ ∞ ♥ ∞ ♥

With my mind I believe my dreams do come true;
Open to receiving the guidance to do the things I do;
With my soul I bring forth the knowledge of ancient times;
Open to knowing truth from deception—to read between the lines.

∞ ♥ ∞ ♥ ∞ ♥ ∞ ♥ ∞ ♥ ∞ ♥ ∞ ♥ ∞ ♥ ∞ ♥ ∞ ♥ ∞ ♥ ∞ ♥ ∞ ♥ ∞ ♥ ∞ ♥ ∞ ♥ ∞ ♥

With my heart I feel an unconditional love;
Open to loving all around me just as I am loved from above;
With my body I walk the path before me;
Open to living a life of happiness & full of blessing always, Believe &
So It Shall Be.

∞ ♥ ∞ ♥ ∞ ♥ ∞ ♥ ∞ ♥ ∞ ♥ ∞ ♥ ∞ ♥ ∞ ♥ ∞ ♥ ∞ ♥ ∞ ♥ ∞ ♥ ∞ ♥ ∞ ♥ ∞ ♥ ∞ ♥

It is within my heart, my soul that I feel a love so strong;
It is within my mind, my imagination (dreams) that I see us together
as we both know with each other we truly belong;
It is within my body I feel the shivers from his touch;
It is within my desires to return his love as given freely & desired so
much.

∞ ♥ ∞ ♥ ∞ ♥ ∞ ♥ ∞ ♥ ∞ ♥ ∞ ♥ ∞ ♥ ∞ ♥ ∞ ♥ ∞ ♥ ∞ ♥ ∞ ♥ ∞ ♥ ∞ ♥ ∞ ♥ ∞ ♥

For the One I seek & find

For the man in this world who honors the needs of my soul, my heart, mind, soul & body seek & find;

Knowing I in return also honor the needs of him completely, his heart. Soul, body & mind;

As equals in our life together, forever walking side by side;

Having true love for each other, intensely unconditional shining so brightly for nothing we hide;

Understanding lovingly each other accepting all we are & yet to be;

For our completion of each other, Two become One for all eternity.

If Hope were a mountain, with Faith to the top I will climb;

If Happiness were an ocean, with Joy in it I will swim within my mind;

If Love were a galaxy, within my Heart & Soul an understanding we are all One I will find.

To understand yourself, all you have ever been, as you are at this very moment, & accepting of all you are yet to become to the depths of your soul;

Creates a love so profound while letting your ego go, then True Love you will find, such a wondrous love for self & for others, before this you could never really know;

Our spirit a gift given for all life, within all creation from One so powerful, immense, always nurturing with Love making us whole;

Without truly loving & accepting oneself we are not capable of Loving or accepting another while on this journey that we now go.

∞ ♥ ∞ ♥ ∞ ♥ ∞ ♥ ∞ ♥ ∞ ♥ ∞ ♥ ∞ ♥ ∞ ♥ ∞ ♥ ∞ ♥ ∞ ♥ ∞ ♥ ∞ ♥ ∞ ♥ ∞ ♥ ∞ ♥

As I awaken this morning from a much needed rest;

With coffee, pen & paper, I begin my daily prayer request;

As I look to the east filled with love within;

I see deer to the south, their journey north they begin;

A new adventure is here, they seemingly say;

Trust you have all you need & remember make some time for play.

∞ ♥ ∞ ♥ ∞ ♥ ∞ ♥ ∞ ♥ ∞ ♥ ∞ ♥ ∞ ♥ ∞ ♥ ∞ ♥ ∞ ♥ ∞ ♥ ∞ ♥ ∞ ♥ ∞ ♥ ∞ ♥ ∞ ♥

A blessing to see & feel, as others show you they care;

Extending their hands & hearts, with you they are always there;

Chasing away fears that had slipped into your mind;

Knowing you are worthy of all your dreams within your heart you find;

My desires & dreams, believing with all that I am, are within reach, coming to me;

With a love so powerful, so intense, with my Father, I am the master, I hold the key.

Making a difference one moment at a time;

Finding a way to let the love within come forth & shine;

Life is an illusion, seen differently by each of us;

Thoughts & dreams becoming reality, with this truth we must have faith & trust.

As I notice so many blessings already in this brand new day;

My heart & mind become one as I begin to pray;

A prayer for all in life for an abundance of happiness, for a lack of strife;

An understanding of self & those that surround you throughout your days;

Acceptance of all blessings as each one comes your way;

A life filled with passions & adventures to find;

Having a faith of such magnitude it fills you, heart, soul & mind;

Trusting you have the ability to cast away all fears & doubt;

Knowing you are loved more than you can comprehend, the love within comes pouring out.

At the break of day I am awake;

In my dreams I already pray for everyone & every things sake;

Running through my mind before I even open my eyes;

"Black as night, White as light, Mighty Father take all that is wrong & make it right", then I see the morning sky;

As this day begins I am filled with peace;

For with each new dawn & new day in life we have a new lease.

∞ ♥ ∞ ♥ ∞ ♥ ∞ ♥ ∞ ♥ ∞ ♥ ∞ ♥ ∞ ♥ ∞ ♥ ∞ ♥ ∞ ♥ ∞ ♥ ∞ ♥ ∞ ♥ ∞ ♥ ∞ ♥ ∞ ♥

Sister moon, full & bright;

Please deliver my prayer upon this night;

To the one I am to love & who loves me back;

For the future filled with joy for nothing we lack;

Brought together to be one;

Always surrounded by light from the stars, you sister moon & our brother sun . . .

Fire light . . .

Moon light . . .

Magic in the air . . .

Love sent to another on the wings of a prayer.

As the fire burns in the hearth warm & bright;

The full moon outside fills this night with light;

My message this day sent to another with love;

Just as instructed by those in heaven above;

For the one who best honors the needs of my soul, I seek & find;

Praying his way to me, he comes with an open heart & an open mind.

This day I have shared with another all that I am;

Hiding nothing, becoming vulnerable, having been told I have nothing to fear;

Stating my desires for the life I dream of with this man;

Believing with all of my heart he will accept all that I am & all I hold dear;

Asking another to walk with me, side by side, hand in hand;

Accepting it will be his freewill choosing with me to be near;

Feeling a strength within him, something I understand;

Trusting the one who has told me, I have no reason to be a-skeered.

∞ ♥ ∞ ♥ ∞ ♥ ∞ ♥ ∞ ♥ ∞ ♥ ∞ ♥ ∞ ♥ ∞ ♥ ∞ ♥ ∞ ♥ ∞ ♥ ∞ ♥ ∞ ♥ ∞ ♥ ∞ ♥

Believing this life brings with it people & things as part of our fate;

Ultimately the outcomes at hand from the choices we make;

Destiny ours to change with each turn on the path we now take;

Understanding the gift of freewill before it is too late.

∞ ♥ ∞ ♥ ∞ ♥ ∞ ♥ ∞ ♥ ∞ ♥ ∞ ♥ ∞ ♥ ∞ ♥ ∞ ♥ ∞ ♥ ∞ ♥ ∞ ♥ ∞ ♥ ∞ ♥ ∞ ♥

A message whispered, so soft, so sweet;

"With patience Little One, your happiness you will meet;

The timing must be right, whether in the day or the night;

To always remember you are surrounded by love & light;

May you find your blessings in this beautiful new day;

Truly there is Love surrounding you always, in every way."

∞ ♥ ∞ ♥ ∞ ♥ ∞ ♥ ∞ ♥ ∞ ♥ ∞ ♥ ∞ ♥ ∞ ♥ ∞ ♥ ∞ ♥ ∞ ♥ ∞ ♥ ∞ ♥ ∞ ♥ ∞ ♥

A worthiness I have found within for the love I seek;
With honesty the truth from my heart I speak;
To share my heart & soul with another I dream;
With much patience I await his acceptance it would seem.

To you I will give completely my heart—for the depths of my love to know;
With you I will share completely my soul—for the depths of my wisdom to know;
To you I will give completely my body—for the depths of its pleasures to know;
With you I will share completely my mind—for the depths of its knowledge to know;
Two becoming One, heart—soul—body—mind;
No greater treasure to ever find.

To know you are worthy of one of life's greatest gifts;
To believe with all your heart in truth you are set free;
To feel your spirit fly as to the heavens it lifts;
To trust in something so magical, so mystical that all is as it should be.

∞ ♥ ∞ ♥ ∞ ♥ ∞ ♥ ∞ ♥ ∞ ♥ ∞ ♥ ∞ ♥ ∞ ♥ ∞ ♥ ∞ ♥ ∞ ♥ ∞ ♥ ∞ ♥ ∞ ♥ ∞ ♥

There is something so royal or regal in all, it's hard to explain;

Like the Lion, King of the Jungle or a black Panther, outwardly different,

yet inwardly the same;

Seeing two beautiful creatures walking side by side;

An acceptance comes naturally, they are who they are, having nothing

to hide;

One as golden as the sun, the other black as night;

A completeness with each other, such a wondrous sight.

Seeing a doe close to the river banks;

Upon seeing her I immediately give my thanks;

Turning away for a moment or two, she disappears from my sight;

A calling for an adventure it seems to find my heart's delights;

Then mystically four more appear;

And again the first one draws near;

And to my surprise before my eyes;

More within the trees now I see revealed from their disguise;

There are seven in all, that I see;

No wait, the eighth just came before me.

The gifts of this world, great & small;

Through unconditional love given to one & all;

This morn I am blessed by the crow, the deer & chickadee;

Through the magic of creation, a new life's adventure of truths is now before me;

Today, a day to celebrate, as was done in the past;

The treasures I seek, it would seem, I have found at last.

To hold a love for so much more;

While holding the key it is easy to unlock the door;

With an open heart & an open mind;

The treasures within lay waiting for you to find.

Many thoughts run through my head;

As I gaze out the window while sitting on my bed;

So many in this life have touched my heart;

Leaving traces of themselves within me, to never part;

Blessings & love given freely by another each day;

Receiving these gifts openly as they come my way.

∞♥∞♥∞♥∞♥∞♥∞♥∞♥∞♥∞♥∞♥∞♥∞♥∞♥∞♥∞♥∞♥∞♥

I feel calmness within me this day;

Trusting all is as it should be in life, in every way;

My dreams & desires I have revealed in love;

Chances in life through Faith in All above.

∞ ♥ ∞ ♥ ∞ ♥ ∞ ♥ ∞ ♥ ∞ ♥ ∞ ♥ ∞ ♥ ∞ ♥ ∞ ♥ ∞ ♥ ∞ ♥ ∞ ♥ ∞ ♥ ∞ ♥ ∞ ♥ ∞ ♥

I wish I could know what it is you think, what it is you feel;

Are the words you sent to me genuine & real;

I wish you happiness in whatever path you choose;

For with my honesty I feel I have everything to gain & nothing to lose;

This world & life are full of mystery everywhere we see;

By looking through Love & Faith we find All is exactly as it should be.

∞ ♥ ∞ ♥ ∞ ♥ ∞ ♥ ∞ ♥ ∞ ♥ ∞ ♥ ∞ ♥ ∞ ♥ ∞ ♥ ∞ ♥ ∞ ♥ ∞ ♥ ∞ ♥ ∞ ♥ ∞ ♥ ∞ ♥

My prayer for you as I go to bed;

May love, peace, happiness fill your heart & head;

An understanding of truths shared;

To be accepted as I am if you truly care.

∞ ♥ ∞ ♥ ∞ ♥ ∞ ♥ ∞ ♥ ∞ ♥ ∞ ♥ ∞ ♥ ∞ ♥ ∞ ♥ ∞ ♥ ∞ ♥ ∞ ♥ ∞ ♥ ∞ ♥ ∞ ♥ ∞ ♥

I, as does the sun, a new day now begin;
To start my day I journey within;
Watching the world come to life outside;
As it is with all, stepping into light, I have nothing to hide.

Thank You Father for this beautiful day;
Thank You for all Blessings sent my way;
Thank You for teaching me of love so true;
Thank You for loving me in all I do.

Father in your love & light I will always be;
Always held in your loving arms—always protecting me;
For all that I hold dear I know the same is true;
Bringing all of creation even closer to you.

As I watch a young deer walking on the river near;
With timidity each step sensing a fear;
Mom shows up not far behind;
Then takes the lead as if saying "Everything is fine."

∞ ♥ ∞ ♥ ∞ ♥ ∞ ♥ ∞ ♥ ∞ ♥ ∞ ♥ ∞ ♥ ∞ ♥ ∞ ♥ ∞ ♥ ∞ ♥ ∞ ♥ ∞ ♥ ∞ ♥ ∞ ♥

Father, this day I ask that you take my doubts & fear;
In love I request your presence & draw you near;
In love & trust I hand over all my fear;
Always knowing within your arms & love, I have nothing to fear as You
hold me near.

∞ ♥ ∞ ♥ ∞ ♥ ∞ ♥ ∞ ♥ ∞ ♥ ∞ ♥ ∞ ♥ ∞ ♥ ∞ ♥ ∞ ♥ ∞ ♥ ∞ ♥ ∞ ♥ ∞ ♥ ∞ ♥

Overwhelmed by a tidal wave of emotions;
Sorrows & joys feeling to me as the depths of an ocean;
Grateful to be able to feel to such depths;
Knowing they must be acknowledged & let go—inside they must not
be kept.

∞ ♥ ∞ ♥ ∞ ♥ ∞ ♥ ∞ ♥ ∞ ♥ ∞ ♥ ∞ ♥ ∞ ♥ ∞ ♥ ∞ ♥ ∞ ♥ ∞ ♥ ∞ ♥ ∞ ♥ ∞ ♥

Wishing you to see me, so look into my eyes;

They are the windows of my soul, there is no disguise;

Accept me as I am, all of me;

Or allow me a blessing & let me be.

With choices that are made are you being true to yourself or due to the way you want others in life, you to perceive;

Do you have enough faith in yourself to trust what is right for you, or look for an outcome you want others to believe;

If you dare to share your heart & soul, the depths of all you are, all you know;

There will be no regrets, no second guessing in any part of life, reaping what you sow.

"When you give of yourself, is it in selfless love or are you looking for a prize?" I know I have asked this before;

Ultimately, if it is a reward you seek, you have just slammed the door;

When in life we look at another seeing a trait they now show;

Whether it is conceived as good or bad, life has just shown us a mirror for that part of ourselves we must acknowledge & come to know;

If there is an expectation of another in this life, something you from them wish to receive;

Do not be fooled, in reality it is an expectation of yourself for something of you with them you must leave;

When seeing someone needing assistance, do you stay & lend a hand;

Or is it easier to walk away, then left alone, there they stand;

To live a life knowing right from wrong;

At times the path may seem lonely & the road itself long;

By giving in all we do, think or say with the love inside, with all of our heart each day;

Treating others as we wish to be treated without judgment, with acceptance in every way;

To understand we must begin everything with the Universal Law in mind;

For in all, including the intent behind it, comes back in kind.

Love & Light shine upon all who draw near;
Casting away shadows of doubt & of fear.

Have you ever felt as if part of your past must be dealt with,
to be able to reach your future . . .

Choices in life, each chance that we take;
Life's lessons we learn & our future we make;
To give with all your heart in everything you do;
Allowing the light to shine upon the shadows making the future
brighter for you.

As I journey onward day in & day out;

Living & loving with all I am, I have no doubt;

Believing in something greater than me leads the way;

Finding treasures while in faith I continue the journey each day.

The world around us changes every second, every day;

Just as each new snowflake changes the earth where it now does lay;

One alone still makes a difference in the place it settles on the ground;

Together with many it creates beauty that is easier to see all around.

∞ ♥ ∞ ♥ ∞ ♥ ∞ ♥ ∞ ♥ ∞ ♥ ∞ ♥ ∞ ♥ ∞ ♥ ∞ ♥ ∞ ♥ ∞ ♥ ∞ ♥ ∞ ♥ ∞ ♥ ∞ ♥

Father, Angels, & Masters above, I call to you for assistance in love;

I ask for your guidance with each step I take this day;

Thank you for holding me near each moment along the way;

I ask that you keep from me all forms of harm;

Thank you for opening my eyes & my heart to see beauty & lifes' charm;

Thank you Father, Angels, Masters one & all;

For hearing my prayer & for answering my call;

Thank you for love that surrounds me in all of my days;

Thank you for the blessings continually sent my way.

∞ ♥ ∞ ♥ ∞ ♥ ∞ ♥ ∞ ♥ ∞ ♥ ∞ ♥ ∞ ♥ ∞ ♥ ∞ ♥ ∞ ♥ ∞ ♥ ∞ ♥ ∞ ♥ ∞ ♥ ∞ ♥

For all that you seek while on the path you walk;

Your spirit through love with your heart & mind will talk;

But the truth that will ring within your ear;

The Ego must be put away if you wish the truth to hear;

To understand there is so much more than just yourself;

Is the key to this world & life unless you wish to be placed on a shelf.

∞ ♥ ∞ ♥ ∞ ♥ ∞ ♥ ∞ ♥ ∞ ♥ ∞ ♥ ∞ ♥ ∞ ♥ ∞ ♥ ∞ ♥ ∞ ♥ ∞ ♥ ∞ ♥ ∞ ♥ ∞ ♥

Have you ever felt as if part of your past must be dealt with,

to be able to reach your future . . .

∞ ♥ ∞ ♥ ∞ ♥ ∞ ♥ ∞ ♥ ∞ ♥ ∞ ♥ ∞ ♥ ∞ ♥ ∞ ♥ ∞ ♥ ∞ ♥ ∞ ♥ ∞ ♥ ∞ ♥ ∞ ♥

Choices in life, each chance that we take;

Life's lessons we learn & our future we make;

To give with all your heart in everything you do;

Allowing the light to shine upon the shadows making the future brighter for you.

∞ ♥ ∞ ♥ ∞ ♥ ∞ ♥ ∞ ♥ ∞ ♥ ∞ ♥ ∞ ♥ ∞ ♥ ∞ ♥ ∞ ♥ ∞ ♥ ∞ ♥ ∞ ♥ ∞ ♥ ∞ ♥

As I journey onward day in & day out;
Living & loving with all I am, I have no doubt;
Believing in something greater than me leads the way;
Finding treasures while in faith I continue the journey each day.
The world around us changes every second, every day;
Just as each new snowflake changes the earth where it now does lay;
One alone still makes a difference in the place it settles on the ground;
Together with many it creates beauty that is easier to see all around.

Father, Angels, & Masters above, I call to you for assistance in love;
I ask for your guidance with each step I take this day;
Thank you for holding me near each moment along the way;
I ask that you keep from me all forms of harm;
Thank you for opening my eyes & my heart to see beauty & lifes' charm;
Thank you Father, Angels, Masters one & all;
For hearing my prayer & for answering my call;
Thank you for love that surrounds me in all of my days;
Thank you for the blessings continually sent my way.

For all that you seek while on the path you walk;

Your spirit through love with your heart & mind will talk;

But the truth that will ring within your ear;

The Ego must be put away if you wish the truth to hear;

To understand there is so much more than just yourself;

Is the key to this world & life unless you wish to be placed on a shelf.

∞ ♥ ∞ ♥ ∞ ♥ ∞ ♥ ∞ ♥ ∞ ♥ ∞ ♥ ∞ ♥ ∞ ♥ ∞ ♥ ∞ ♥ ∞ ♥ ∞ ♥ ∞ ♥ ∞ ♥ ∞ ♥ ∞ ♥

Each soul having many facets allowing to shine;

From the depths within, the secrets held, we need seek & find;

To share all that is within, one must only gaze into the windows of the soul to see;

For the eyes reveal much, always in truth which ultimately will set us free;

Thus accepting another just as they are & all they are meant to be;

Able to see profuse Love & Light—it is the same within you & within me.

∞ ♥ ∞ ♥ ∞ ♥ ∞ ♥ ∞ ♥ ∞ ♥ ∞ ♥ ∞ ♥ ∞ ♥ ∞ ♥ ∞ ♥ ∞ ♥ ∞ ♥ ∞ ♥ ∞ ♥ ∞ ♥ ∞ ♥

Dare to dream your dreams & search the depths within;

A wondrous adventure in life will begin;

Trust with your heart & to it be true;

A beautiful life will open up to you.

∞ ♥ ∞ ♥ ∞ ♥ ∞ ♥ ∞ ♥ ∞ ♥ ∞ ♥ ∞ ♥ ∞ ♥ ∞ ♥ ∞ ♥ ∞ ♥ ∞ ♥ ∞ ♥ ∞ ♥ ∞ ♥ ∞ ♥

Father of All, Master of None;
Love is the Key, that sets us Free;
One for All, All for One.

Who or what in life is your Master?
Who or What controls you—
your thoughts,
your words, written & spoken,
your actions?
Is it a person?
Is it money or greed?
Is it loneliness or anger?

For me, the answer is simply LOVE
I have no Master
I am the Master of ME.

A sadness is within me, my heart knowing Winters' beauty shall soon be gone;

A joy I also feel, knowing Spring & new beginnings will appear before too long;

Then again the warmth of the Summers' sun new adventures will call as the season is begun;

And to slow down again as Autumn makes its way back as we follow the journey of the sun.

Preparing for Winter once more, its' beauty to return again, the circle complete as nothing is left undone. ☺

The rhythm of the flicker tapping at a tree;

Reminds me of the rhythms that surround you & me;

The rhythm of the heart, the rhythm of love;

Keeping life in motion with the rhythm above;

The rhythm of the seasons & the beauty that can be found;

Becoming One with the rhythm of All is where the blessings abound.

Trust yourself & your heart within;

To follow your heart is the only way to win;

The strength inside you will be a surprise;

As you change the world right before your eyes;

Ask the questions you wish to know;

Be open to the answers throughout the days as you go;

Believe with all you are, with all your heart;

From Your true path you will never part.

So many questions run through my mind;

All of he answers lie within waiting for me to find;

With Love & Gratitude my heart is filled each day;

Ah, before my eyes, such gifts of beauty & splendor are here to stay;

In awe of the magical mysteries of this earth;

Feeling very fortunate from the day of my birth.

Have you ever wondered why certain people appear or disappear in your life;

Some remaining, to walk with you in happiness & strife;

Others departing, perhaps after only moments or maybe even years, leaving traces upon your mind, heart or soul just the same;

Most cases teaching a lesson whether great or small, in acceptance, responsibility, seeing something in yourself or karma by another name;

Ever notice when we like or dislike a trait of another it is that within our self we must face;

Everyone & everything in our life happening as it should, being perfect in the timing, the people & the place.

∞ ♥ ∞ ♥ ∞ ♥ ∞ ♥ ∞ ♥ ∞ ♥ ∞ ♥ ∞ ♥ ∞ ♥ ∞ ♥ ∞ ♥ ∞ ♥ ∞ ♥ ∞ ♥ ∞ ♥ ∞ ♥

What dreams may come when we allow our heart to lead the way;

What joy & laughter will fill our life while on our path we stay;

What blessings will touch your soul to the depth beyond that which we comprehend;

What love will you allow to touch your heart, mind, body & soul from beginning to end.

∞ ♥ ∞ ♥ ∞ ♥ ∞ ♥ ∞ ♥ ∞ ♥ ∞ ♥ ∞ ♥ ∞ ♥ ∞ ♥ ∞ ♥ ∞ ♥ ∞ ♥ ∞ ♥ ∞ ♥ ∞ ♥

Sometimes you can feel a love for another as if you are not complete, not whole;

Through the choices made in this life, sometimes you win when you lose, sometimes you lose when you win;

Be true to your heart in every choice you make, remembering with each chance or risk you take, love will be your guide on the life path you now stroll;

Give all of yourself in everything you do allowing the love & light to come shining through in every moment of every day as you begin.

∞ ♥ ∞ ♥ ∞ ♥ ∞ ♥ ∞ ♥ ∞ ♥ ∞ ♥ ∞ ♥ ∞ ♥ ∞ ♥ ∞ ♥ ∞ ♥ ∞ ♥ ∞ ♥ ∞ ♥ ∞ ♥

This morning a little grey squirrel taught me a lesson in trust;

In amazement I watched it take a leap of faith, for Faith was a must;

It climbed to the top of my maple tree;

And without hesitation jumped to another tree branch perfectly;

Trust & Faith a must; Believing in yourself, you have the strength to always take that Leap in Faith!

∞ ♥ ∞ ♥ ∞ ♥ ∞ ♥ ∞ ♥ ∞ ♥ ∞ ♥ ∞ ♥ ∞ ♥ ∞ ♥ ∞ ♥ ∞ ♥ ∞ ♥ ∞ ♥ ∞ ♥ ∞ ♥

Each day in love I find in nature the lessons it brings;

My favorite, the sunrise—making my mind, heart & soul to sing;

New beginnings a gift with each new day;

Take a leap in faith & allow the blessings to come your way;

Believe & it shall be;

Love & Light is always surrounding thee.

Grateful for the gifts I have to share;

Grateful for the love to show that I care;

Grateful for truth & light that guides my way;

Grateful for innumerable blessings every moment of every day;

Grateful for wisdom & knowledge that comes from within;

Grateful for the soft & gentle whispers as my days begin.

∞ ♥ ∞ ♥ ∞ ♥ ∞ ♥ ∞ ♥ ∞ ♥ ∞ ♥ ∞ ♥ ∞ ♥ ∞ ♥ ∞ ♥ ∞ ♥ ∞ ♥ ∞ ♥ ∞ ♥

Always remember you are loved, valued! Not everyone in this world
will understand all of you & that is okay, because they are not supposed
to. Let your heart be your guide through the wisdom of your soul
revealing to your mind all you need to know.

Blessings Sunshine ☺

∞ ♥ ∞ ♥ ∞ ♥ ∞ ♥ ∞ ♥ ∞ ♥ ∞ ♥ ∞ ♥ ∞ ♥ ∞ ♥ ∞ ♥ ∞ ♥ ∞ ♥ ∞ ♥ ∞ ♥

Each day as I journey I hold something beautiful within my mind;
Searching with truth in my heart the one who best honors my soul, I
seek & find.

∞ ♥ ∞ ♥ ∞ ♥ ∞ ♥ ∞ ♥ ∞ ♥ ∞ ♥ ∞ ♥ ∞ ♥ ∞ ♥ ∞ ♥ ∞ ♥ ∞ ♥ ∞ ♥ ∞ ♥

In living your life, to yourself be true;

For we are responsible to ourselves in all we think, say or do;

The only one in life we are accountable to & live with is our self;

It matters not, the opinions of others, approval or disapproval about how we live & what we do, so place them up on a shelf;

Some will say how they see things then turn & walk away;

It seems to me it is their ego taking control, letting their actions sway;

Letting go of the ego means no strings attached to anything we do;

Without expectations of return or repayment of what we give, our true self comes shining through;

That is when we need to stand firm in our beliefs, staying strong & live our life as we know we are to live;

Our light within shining as brightly if not brighter than before, giving all we have to give;

Dare to be different, live your life with no regrets, no guilt, no shame, letting all see you as you truly are;

Life will take care of your every need & leads you to people who love & accept everything about you, just as you are;

***Let your light shine, do not change or hide who you are to please another—

Make them uncomfortable if that is what it takes—

The only one you need to answer to & live with in this life is yourself.

So treat others as you wish to be treated, judgment of another will only lead to being judged yourself, live life to the fullest in honesty & love, harming no other & life you shall find will be filled with much delight.

There are moments when steps must be taken as one is told;
There are moments when one must step back & watch life unfold;
Trusting all is as it should be every moment, every way;
Letting go of control, allowing Love to shine & guide each day;
For everything in life there is a reason;
For everything in life there is a season.

∞ ♥ ∞ ♥ ∞ ♥ ∞ ♥ ∞ ♥ ∞ ♥ ∞ ♥ ∞ ♥ ∞ ♥ ∞ ♥ ∞ ♥ ∞ ♥ ∞ ♥ ∞ ♥ ∞ ♥ ∞ ♥ ∞ ♥

There is a calmness in the air this day;
A peacefulness that feels it is here to stay.

∞ ♥ ∞ ♥ ∞ ♥ ∞ ♥ ∞ ♥ ∞ ♥ ∞ ♥ ∞ ♥ ∞ ♥ ∞ ♥ ∞ ♥ ∞ ♥ ∞ ♥ ∞ ♥ ∞ ♥ ∞ ♥ ∞ ♥

Staying up late into the night;
Talking with friends, then sleeping through mornings light;
Having extended an invitation to assist another;
Funny, how my Father still works life out to sit with a sister & a brother;
His timing, always in order with perfection;
There are no coincidences, Only connections.

∞ ♥ ∞ ♥ ∞ ♥ ∞ ♥ ∞ ♥ ∞ ♥ ∞ ♥ ∞ ♥ ∞ ♥ ∞ ♥ ∞ ♥ ∞ ♥ ∞ ♥ ∞ ♥ ∞ ♥ ∞ ♥

Upon coming home after work a precious gift I did find;

A beautiful rose on my table, a gesture so loving, so kind;

A confirmation I am loved, touching my heart, my soul, my mind;

Reminded as always, what you give, you receive through the ties that bind.

New & glorious day has begun;

Old friends return singing their song for me to hear as it is sung;

Mixed emotions, sorrow & excitement, I feel inside;

As Winter is readying to leave, to again hide;

Opening the way for New Beginnings as Spring walks in;

With many new adventures my days will begin.

∞ ♥ ∞ ♥ ∞ ♥ ∞ ♥ ∞ ♥ ∞ ♥ ∞ ♥ ∞ ♥ ∞ ♥ ∞ ♥ ∞ ♥ ∞ ♥ ∞ ♥ ∞ ♥ ∞ ♥

Having awakened this morning exhausted, wanting to stay in bed all day;

So very unlike me to allow a beautiful day slip away;

Gazing out my windows at Narnia once more;

Sadness touches me, as it will soon be gone ending as it always has before.

∞ ♥ ∞ ♥ ∞ ♥ ∞ ♥ ∞ ♥ ∞ ♥ ∞ ♥ ∞ ♥ ∞ ♥ ∞ ♥ ∞ ♥ ∞ ♥ ∞ ♥ ∞ ♥ ∞ ♥

There is something inside, a sadness I feel;
I am on the outside looking in, for with these feelings I must now deal;
To uncover truths, this journey I now make;
To find love, light & joy within undoubtedly a risk I will take.

Changes in life, changes in me;
Changes, changes, everywhere I look, that is all I see;
Changes of the heart, which way will I go?
Changes through truth & love, faithfully in your life will show.

A restful night had been my plight;
To sleep while surrounded with love & light;
Blessed with sweet dreams that stayed with me through the night;
Awakened by the warmth of the sun to a beautiful new sight.

∞ ♥ ∞ ♥ ∞ ♥ ∞ ♥ ∞ ♥ ∞ ♥ ∞ ♥ ∞ ♥ ∞ ♥ ∞ ♥ ∞ ♥ ∞ ♥ ∞ ♥ ∞ ♥ ∞ ♥ ∞ ♥

Dreams can be very Real;
Yet Real can be very much like a Dream.

Gifts received in the most unexpected ways;
"Be careful for what you wish for, you just might get it", an old wives
tales says;
A heartfelt request I recently sent up above;
To be surrounded with truth, protection, light & love.

In 3 days time a rose & candle were left for me;
Friendship & truth (yellow rose), protection, light & love (St Michael
candle) as answers to my prayers for me to see.

A brand new start with a brand new day;

Finding love within me is constant & always here to stay;

Trusting in a power so much greater than me;

Believing all in life works out, just as it is meant to be;

Cared for by one through the hands of so many;

At this moment in time, no fears, no worries, I haven't got any.

∞ ♥ ∞ ♥ ∞ ♥ ∞ ♥ ∞ ♥ ∞ ♥ ∞ ♥ ∞ ♥ ∞ ♥ ∞ ♥ ∞ ♥ ∞ ♥ ∞ ♥ ∞ ♥ ∞ ♥ ∞ ♥

A Dream can seem very much like reality;

Yet Reality can seem very much like a dream . . .

May your Dreams be spectacular & your Reality all your dreams come true.

∞ ♥ ∞ ♥ ∞ ♥ ∞ ♥ ∞ ♥ ∞ ♥ ∞ ♥ ∞ ♥ ∞ ♥ ∞ ♥ ∞ ♥ ∞ ♥ ∞ ♥ ∞ ♥ ∞ ♥ ∞ ♥

Blessed without measure in this life of mine;

To find a treasure of love that transcends all space & time;

Cared for by many that are guided by One;

For those that do listen, they outshine the sun.

∞ ♥ ∞ ♥ ∞ ♥ ∞ ♥ ∞ ♥ ∞ ♥ ∞ ♥ ∞ ♥ ∞ ♥ ∞ ♥ ∞ ♥ ∞ ♥ ∞ ♥ ∞ ♥ ∞ ♥ ∞ ♥

To live a life with No Regrets, No Shame, No Guilt;

Allows us to look back in awe & wonder of the life we built;

To live a life with No Judgment of others, No Blame;

Allows us to receive what we give, learning to love unconditionally is the name of the game;

To live life to the fullest in love each day;

Allows us to harm no other in any form, in any way.

There is much knowledge in this world given to man (woman) from above;

To be taken within & deciphered with love;

As a way of controlling others, some use deceit;

There are some with an understanding of the secrets, those you know when you meet;

The key to this knowledge is given to all, it sits in the palm of your hand;

Use the key, unlock the mysteries, the secrets & begin to completely accept & understand.

As I sit & look upon the beauty that lies before me;

Taking it all in, every detail I see;

My thoughts travel to the future, to days yet to be;

Changing my vision to watching old friends who every spring come to visit me;

Loons, mysterious in their own right, swim in the rivers' thawing waters, I see;

With a smile, knowing everything happens just as it is meant to be.

Look within my eyes, I will share with you my soul;

For there I hide nothing, my loves, my dreams, my desires, my fears, all to you I will show;

Taking a risk on life through trust & faith I attain my goal;

To be true to myself, therefore truthful with all is the best path I know.

My heart aches with an emptiness only one may fill;

With every beat it longs for him to be with me still;

A love held for an eternity to me it seems;

For only now may I see him within my dreams;

From the depth of my soul feelings of a love that transcends all space & time;

In faith I hold a belief my future holds this love that is mine.

A desire to dance beneath the stars & full moon;

With the man who has held my heart forever & a day;

My soul cries out that we may be together again very soon;

For once again there will be a longing within us both, for in loves arms

to stay.

∞ ♥ ∞ ♥ ∞ ♥ ∞ ♥ ∞ ♥ ∞ ♥ ∞ ♥ ∞ ♥ ∞ ♥ ∞ ♥ ∞ ♥ ∞ ♥ ∞ ♥ ∞ ♥ ∞ ♥ ∞ ♥

This morning as I reluctantly opened my eyes;

I was able to see the sun kiss the morning skies;

To also see deer, turkeys & a hawk with a snake fly by;

As if a voice within had aroused me to witness such things;

My heart & soul join in as the morning birds begin to sing;

Life has many blessings with each new day it brings.

∞ ♥ ∞ ♥ ∞ ♥ ∞ ♥ ∞ ♥ ∞ ♥ ∞ ♥ ∞ ♥ ∞ ♥ ∞ ♥ ∞ ♥ ∞ ♥ ∞ ♥ ∞ ♥ ∞ ♥ ∞ ♥

Sometimes we stumble, sometimes we fall;

At times in life, it is the bottom we must reach before we can see it all;

But we are never alone on this journey we take;

We are always guided to the choices we may make;

It can be an uphill climb & worth each step of the way;

When we reach the top, that's where we will long to stay;

"Faith makes things possible . . . Not easy"

∞ ♥ ∞ ♥ ∞ ♥ ∞ ♥ ∞ ♥ ∞ ♥ ∞ ♥ ∞ ♥ ∞ ♥ ∞ ♥ ∞ ♥ ∞ ♥ ∞ ♥ ∞ ♥ ∞ ♥ ∞ ♥

With a gentleness, love is whispered in my ear;
Creating a calmness within as I release all fear;
In faith I continue to move forward now;
Believing everything will be right somehow.

∞ ♥ ∞ ♥ ∞ ♥ ∞ ♥ ∞ ♥ ∞ ♥ ∞ ♥ ∞ ♥ ∞ ♥ ∞ ♥ ∞ ♥ ∞ ♥ ∞ ♥ ∞ ♥ ∞ ♥ ∞ ♥ ∞ ♥

There is so much I want to say, so much I want to share;
I desire to reach out to someone & show how much I care;
The door that once was open feels as though it now closes from the
other side;
With sorrow & heartache, to your wishes, I will abide.

∞ ♥ ∞ ♥ ∞ ♥ ∞ ♥ ∞ ♥ ∞ ♥ ∞ ♥ ∞ ♥ ∞ ♥ ∞ ♥ ∞ ♥ ∞ ♥ ∞ ♥ ∞ ♥ ∞ ♥ ∞ ♥ ∞ ♥

Through an open heart & an open mind;
This world, this life holds many treasures to find;
Like the birds of the air or the creatures of the earth;
We too are loved & cared for from the moment of our birth.

∞ ♥ ∞ ♥ ∞ ♥ ∞ ♥ ∞ ♥ ∞ ♥ ∞ ♥ ∞ ♥ ∞ ♥ ∞ ♥ ∞ ♥ ∞ ♥ ∞ ♥ ∞ ♥ ∞ ♥ ∞ ♥ ∞ ♥

Thank you Father . . .

I am grateful to be filled with so much love, at times I literally cannot breathe,

because it takes my breath away;

I am grateful for the sorrow & pain, because it reminds me of all the love that forever with me will stay.

I Love You Forever & a Day ☺

Without heartache we cannot know the intense love held within our heart;

Without sorrow & pain we cannot know the happiness & joys this life holds;

Without difficulties & hardships we cannot know that strength & courage we have;

All allowing us to spread our wings & grow;

Hope everyone has a beautiful day, filled with many moments that take your breath away, may you find within whatever is needed each step of the way. Hugs

I pray for love, protection & truth with all of creation to be;

I believe it is the love & truth that protects us & sets us free.

The earth is changing every moment, every day;
She is waking from her slumber in a miraculous way;
All of nature is transforming from the earth to the skies;
A blessing indeed unfolding right before my eyes.

Be true to yourself, follow your heart, let it be your guide;
A life of truth, love & light is my choice, whether alone or with another
walking side by side;
My heart is in the hands of my Father above;
Trusting I am always in His care & protection in love;
With each step on my journey, each choice I freely make;
Each moment in my life, understanding the impact as I freely give &
freely take.

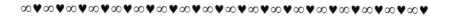

Sunshine & rainbows are everywhere;

Excitement & magic fills the air;

With each step we take a new adventure is begun;

As if life itself is saying "Take a chance, follow your heart, drink it all in & have some fun!"

In living your life, to yourself being true;

It matters not the opinions of others about how you live or what you do;

Some will say how they see things then turn & walk away;

It seems to me it is their ego taking control, letting their actions sway;

That is when we need to stand firm in our beliefs staying strong & live our life as we know we are to live;

Our light within shining as brightly, if not brighter then before, giving all we have to give.

Letting go of the ego means, no strings attached to anything we do;

Without expectations our true self always comes shining through;

So live your life with no regrets, letting all see you as you truly are;

Life takes care of your very need & leads you to people who love &
accept you just as you are;

Let your light shine, do not change or hide who you are

—make them uncomfortable if that is what it takes,

only one you need to answer to & live with is yourself,

so enjoy life, live to the fullest, harming no other & life is filled with
much delight. ☺

∞ ♥ ∞ ♥ ∞ ♥ ∞ ♥ ∞ ♥ ∞ ♥ ∞ ♥ ∞ ♥ ∞ ♥ ∞ ♥ ∞ ♥ ∞ ♥ ∞ ♥ ∞ ♥ ∞ ♥ ∞ ♥

There is a rhythm to life . . . Can you feel the beat?

∞ ♥ ∞ ♥ ∞ ♥ ∞ ♥ ∞ ♥ ∞ ♥ ∞ ♥ ∞ ♥ ∞ ♥ ∞ ♥ ∞ ♥ ∞ ♥ ∞ ♥ ∞ ♥ ∞ ♥ ∞ ♥

Whispers, so soft, so gentle, so clear;

Whispers of love, quietly spoken are what I hear;

I will whisper to you, will you whisper to me;

As life gently whispers, "all is fine, trust that everything is exactly as it
is meant to be."

∞ ♥ ∞ ♥ ∞ ♥ ∞ ♥ ∞ ♥ ∞ ♥ ∞ ♥ ∞ ♥ ∞ ♥ ∞ ♥ ∞ ♥ ∞ ♥ ∞ ♥ ∞ ♥ ∞ ♥ ∞ ♥

The waters of the river begin to flow freely once more;

Spring is walking quietly through Winters' door;

There is movement within the water, ripples I now see;

Soon the Loons shall return for a time, this place their home it too will be;

Quietly watching nature transform before my eyes;

Changes within life are just blessings in disguise.

Life is mysterious & magical in a way;

Remember to take time to smell the roses & see their beauty every day;

Being mindful that with the rose, each has a thorn;

And in carelessness the flesh may be torn.

My thoughts drift to many I hold dear to my heart;

Grateful for lifes' blessings & challenges that bring us closer than before;

Moments shared, whether with tears or laughter, memories remain never to part;

Life is mysterious & magical in a way, it leaves us wanting more.

There was a gentle man at work, Gabow is his name;

After yesterday, his life will never be the same;

He lost a son to a bullet flying through the air;

I believe he is returning home, Somalia, as he is needed there;

A connection had been made between he & I;

A friendship that grew as each day went by;

His soul is kind & he is pure in heart;

He called me "sister" in his language right from the start;

My heartfelt sadness made tears fill my eyes;

My thoughts & prayers are with him as homeward he flies.

Through the heartache of another, yesterday I was gently reminded life changes in an instant;

I am grateful for all I have, family, friends, home & even all the critters including the two I call pets;

I am grateful for love & friendship as well as so much more;

I am grateful that whatever I do or wherever I go, it is done with all my heart;

Remember to tell all those you hold dear, how much you love them;

And when you say "I love you", mean it!

We do not always know what tomorrow may bring.

Each day holds treasures for us to find;

The secret, we must search with our heart, soul & mind.

Just days ago the river was a pathway for deer, made of ice;

Today flowing freely it is a Loons paradise;

Such beauty, such grace, in nature I see;

My old friends have returned for a time, to dance upon the waters

before me.

My dreams & desires are held within my heart;

To have a love in my life, knowing we never will part;

An adventure each day in the life we will live;

Adoration & love to each other we will give;

Spring has now arrived, a time for new beginnings is in the air;

Trustingly I continue each day filled with faith, in a love to share.

∞♥∞♥∞♥∞♥∞♥∞♥∞♥∞♥∞♥∞♥∞♥∞♥∞♥∞♥∞♥∞♥

The waters of life, move quickly it seems;

Take time each day to believe & manifest your dreams.

∞ ♥ ∞ ♥ ∞ ♥ ∞ ♥ ∞ ♥ ∞ ♥ ∞ ♥ ∞ ♥ ∞ ♥ ∞ ♥ ∞ ♥ ∞ ♥ ∞ ♥ ∞ ♥ ∞ ♥ ∞ ♥

There are those times that I fret, times that I worry;

Forgetting things happen in there own time, I get in a hurry;

Believing all events in life are there for reasons;

Changes happen within, just as we have changes of the seasons;

It is difficult to trust we are exactly where we are meant to be;

But without the events, the changes, you would not be you & I would

not be me.

∞ ♥ ∞ ♥ ∞ ♥ ∞ ♥ ∞ ♥ ∞ ♥ ∞ ♥ ∞ ♥ ∞ ♥ ∞ ♥ ∞ ♥ ∞ ♥ ∞ ♥ ∞ ♥ ∞ ♥ ∞ ♥

Time: where does it go? Why does it stand still? Why does it fly by?

Time is an illusion, so live life to the fullest & you will see why.

∞ ♥ ∞ ♥ ∞ ♥ ∞ ♥ ∞ ♥ ∞ ♥ ∞ ♥ ∞ ♥ ∞ ♥ ∞ ♥ ∞ ♥ ∞ ♥ ∞ ♥ ∞ ♥ ∞ ♥ ∞ ♥

I long to show you the world that I see;

Come talk a while & walk with me;

Take a chance on life, maybe true love will be found;

Listen closely, two hearts beating as one, in unison they pound;

Gazing into your eyes, I will see who you truly are;

Your soul shining as bright as the morning star;

My heart, soul, mind & body, long for you to be near;

Forever & a day your love I will hold dear;

I promise to hold you in my arms, protect you with truth & love;

For you to me are heaven sent, a gift from above.

Deep within me, passion like a wild fire does burn;

For there is one in this world my mind, body, heart & soul does yearn;

There is an emptiness inside without you near;

With every heartbeat, I pray my voice you will hear;

I give you my nights, I give you my days;

For true love I have found, transcends all time & space forever & always.

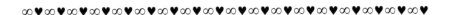

Outside this morning is where I desired to be;
So grabbed my coffee & out to the deck it went with me;
I sat in silence looking all around;
Listening to nature speak is a joy I have found;
As the river rambles by I listen to her own sweet song;
Then the voices of the birds join in & sing along;
Serenity at my sanctuary it is one of the greatest treasures I have found;
Blessed by all through sight & sound.

∞♥∞♥∞♥∞♥∞♥∞♥∞♥∞♥∞♥∞♥∞♥∞♥∞♥∞♥∞♥∞♥∞♥

Each day I escape for a time into a world of my own;
A place where wonders, mystery & magic is known;
As I open my eyes & open my heart, I am grateful each day;
For an amazing world, the magic & love in my life that is here to stay.

∞♥∞♥∞♥∞♥∞♥∞♥∞♥∞♥∞♥∞♥∞♥∞♥∞♥∞♥∞♥∞♥∞♥

Blessed beyond measure, my entire life it seems;
Watching my reality emerge from my wildest dreams.

∞♥∞♥∞♥∞♥∞♥∞♥∞♥∞♥∞♥∞♥∞♥∞♥∞♥∞♥∞♥∞♥∞♥

Life can have difficulties at times it seems;

Making us doubt as it tears at our dreams;

Or we can find the strength & courage within;

In letting go we can find—when we win we lose but when we lose we win;

In facing fears we learn to grow;

If we run away, they surface again, from ourselves there is no where to go.

It feels as if Ireland has come to me;

At first it was the sun but now it is fog I see;

In some strange way it gives me comfort, fills me with peace, heart, mind & soul;

My prayers, my wishes for all is your inner peace you may also find;

Happy St. Patrick's Day

May each moment hold blessings for you in every way.

Irish Blessing

May your troubles be few

Your blessings be more and

Nothing but happiness come through your door.

∞♥∞♥∞♥∞♥∞♥∞♥∞♥∞♥∞♥∞♥∞♥∞♥∞♥∞♥∞♥∞♥

There are some thoughts, a friend once did share;

Desiring to understand life's journey, life's plan, but that is no longer there;

If truths are revealed regarding akashic records or the book of life, they be known;

Wouldn't egos take over, there by not allowing the growth of our soul to be sown;

It seems it is best to take a leap in faith, letting come what may;

Fulfilling our lifes' purpose, growing from challenges & blessings met everyday;

After all, it is all about the journey not the destination in life;

Including love, truth, happiness, sorrow, pain & challenges or strife.

**Note: definitions looked up in Webster's Dictionary

Life—it is all about the journey, not the destination, the destination is already known

Journey—a traveling from one place to another

Life—1) that property of plants & animals (ending in death) which makes it possible for them to take in food, get energy from it, grow, etc

2) a state of having this property

3) a human being

4) living things collectively

5) the time a person or thing is alive or exists

May you be surrounded by love every moment of every day;

With an abundance of sunshine & rainbows to come your way;

At the end of the rainbow may you seek your pot of gold;

Finding all your treasures & dreams within, it truly does hold.

If given a choice & truths may be known;

Would you look at the Akashic records, the pages of the Book of Life shown;

If this knowledge you held, would you have the strength & courage to stay true to the life path that lays before you;

Taking the heartaches, sorrows, pain & challenges still ahead as well as the love, happiness, peace & joys that comes with each day new.

∞ ♥ ∞ ♥ ∞ ♥ ∞ ♥ ∞ ♥ ∞ ♥ ∞ ♥ ∞ ♥ ∞ ♥ ∞ ♥ ∞ ♥ ∞ ♥ ∞ ♥ ∞ ♥ ∞ ♥ ∞ ♥

Mesmerized as sunlight dances on the water before me now;

Or seeing the starlit sky on a moonless night;

Like a moth to a flame, always drawn to the light somehow;

In awe & wonder I get lost in such beauty & am filled with delight.

∞ ♥ ∞ ♥ ∞ ♥ ∞ ♥ ∞ ♥ ∞ ♥ ∞ ♥ ∞ ♥ ∞ ♥ ∞ ♥ ∞ ♥ ∞ ♥ ∞ ♥ ∞ ♥ ∞ ♥ ∞ ♥

May you be filled with love & light each day;

Allowing you to chase all of life's shadows away;

Find some time to let your inner child come out & play;

Truly it is the simple things in life that brings a happiness that is here

to stay.

∞ ♥ ∞ ♥ ∞ ♥ ∞ ♥ ∞ ♥ ∞ ♥ ∞ ♥ ∞ ♥ ∞ ♥ ∞ ♥ ∞ ♥ ∞ ♥ ∞ ♥ ∞ ♥ ∞ ♥ ∞ ♥

Last night a scent of rain was in the air;

If it sprinkled or down poured I did not care;

How I wished you were there.

∞ ♥ ∞ ♥ ∞ ♥ ∞ ♥ ∞ ♥ ∞ ♥ ∞ ♥ ∞ ♥ ∞ ♥ ∞ ♥ ∞ ♥ ∞ ♥ ∞ ♥ ∞ ♥ ∞ ♥ ∞ ♥

I, like the river, move along each day;

My course in life, predetermined in some way;

Just like the river, flowing within its' banks, made of dirt & clay;

A pace steady & true with an occasional outburst, being rapid & fierce,

yet remaining on the path I am meant to stay.

∞ ♥ ∞ ♥ ∞ ♥ ∞ ♥ ∞ ♥ ∞ ♥ ∞ ♥ ∞ ♥ ∞ ♥ ∞ ♥ ∞ ♥ ∞ ♥ ∞ ♥ ∞ ♥ ∞ ♥ ∞ ♥

The first day of spring has finally come;

A time for changes is now at hand;

Now is the time to see our hopes, wishes & dreams, thrive & flourish;

As we draw ourselves out of winters' hibernation, noticing a newness in life has begun;

Even the earth has lost her blanket of white that covered the land;

It is time of new beginnings, new growth, new opportunities, like the phoenix rising out of the ashes—letting love & light your heart, mind & soul nourish.

Yesterday holds nothing for me except my memories;

But my tomorrow holds my dreams, through faith they become my realities.

There are days that my heart & soul aches beyond anything I have ever known;

But yet I believe in a magic in this life, for many blessings I have been shown;

From a depth within me, my dreams are kept alive, for one day I have faith I will reap what I have sown;

To live a life filled with unconditional love as an adventure leading into the familiar yet unknown.

My heart longs for someone dear;

My mind calls to him, yet I wonder if what I say, does he hear;

My body desires him, with him I wish to be near;

My soul misses him, I want him to be here.

∞ ♥ ∞ ♥ ∞ ♥ ∞ ♥ ∞ ♥ ∞ ♥ ∞ ♥ ∞ ♥ ∞ ♥ ∞ ♥ ∞ ♥ ∞ ♥ ∞ ♥ ∞ ♥ ∞ ♥ ∞ ♥

As I watch the sunrise, I give many thanks for the day;

And all the beauty & blessings that come my way;

Before me, I see some Loons, noticing they skim across the shallows &
dive where the waters are deep;

I wonder is that a fundamental secret they keep.

∞ ♥ ∞ ♥ ∞ ♥ ∞ ♥ ∞ ♥ ∞ ♥ ∞ ♥ ∞ ♥ ∞ ♥ ∞ ♥ ∞ ♥ ∞ ♥ ∞ ♥ ∞ ♥ ∞ ♥ ∞ ♥

A prayer last night my heart did hold;

For my heart to be filled with love replacing the emptiness inside;

My prayer has been answered through nature, I am told;

As I continue to follow my heart always, it will be my guide.

∞ ♥ ∞ ♥ ∞ ♥ ∞ ♥ ∞ ♥ ∞ ♥ ∞ ♥ ∞ ♥ ∞ ♥ ∞ ♥ ∞ ♥ ∞ ♥ ∞ ♥ ∞ ♥ ∞ ♥ ∞ ♥

Just outside my window, in a nearby tree;

My friend, Hawk, has come to visit me;

It sits there as a sentry, a guardian from above;

Reminding me, I am always protected & surrounded with love.

After a restful night;

To wake with the morning light;

There is a calmness in the air;

Around me, I feel it everywhere;

Always grateful for this life, I am blessed to live;

Reminded once more, everything comes full circle—you get back what you give.

There is so much in this world to see & do;

Many adventures laid out before me & you;

Some will be near, some will be far;

Perhaps some are the answers to a wish upon a star.

∞♥∞♥∞♥∞♥∞♥∞♥∞♥∞♥∞♥∞♥∞♥∞♥∞♥∞♥∞♥∞♥

My mind runs rampant with thoughts of you;
So grateful you are in my life, a dream come true;
Always my equal whether we are near or far;
My heart, my love goes with you wherever you are.

∞ ♥ ∞ ♥ ∞ ♥ ∞ ♥ ∞ ♥ ∞ ♥ ∞ ♥ ∞ ♥ ∞ ♥ ∞ ♥ ∞ ♥ ∞ ♥ ∞ ♥ ∞ ♥ ∞ ♥ ∞ ♥

There is something or someone in this world that I seek to find;
A man who best honors the needs of my soul, loving, gentle & kind;
The one who will share my dream each & every day;
A love of two, yet one, in every way.

∞ ♥ ∞ ♥ ∞ ♥ ∞ ♥ ∞ ♥ ∞ ♥ ∞ ♥ ∞ ♥ ∞ ♥ ∞ ♥ ∞ ♥ ∞ ♥ ∞ ♥ ∞ ♥ ∞ ♥ ∞ ♥

A beautiful day, leading into a beautiful night;
Everything in life feels perfectly right;
My heart searches for something as if on a quest;
My heart I will follow, for me & my life, it always knows best.

∞ ♥ ∞ ♥ ∞ ♥ ∞ ♥ ∞ ♥ ∞ ♥ ∞ ♥ ∞ ♥ ∞ ♥ ∞ ♥ ∞ ♥ ∞ ♥ ∞ ♥ ∞ ♥ ∞ ♥ ∞ ♥

I believe in miracles, I believe dreams do come true;

I believe everything happens for a reason, everything we do;

I believe all will be made right while remaining on our path in life;

I believe many blessings unfold with each little event of strife.

∞ ♥ ∞ ♥ ∞ ♥ ∞ ♥ ∞ ♥ ∞ ♥ ∞ ♥ ∞ ♥ ∞ ♥ ∞ ♥ ∞ ♥ ∞ ♥ ∞ ♥ ∞ ♥ ∞ ♥ ∞ ♥

My thoughts this day are even a mystery to me;

Everything & nothing at the same time I see;

Life at its' grandest yet simplest form I seem to understand as it is meant to be;

Still my thoughts this day are even a mystery to me.

∞ ♥ ∞ ♥ ∞ ♥ ∞ ♥ ∞ ♥ ∞ ♥ ∞ ♥ ∞ ♥ ∞ ♥ ∞ ♥ ∞ ♥ ∞ ♥ ∞ ♥ ∞ ♥ ∞ ♥ ∞ ♥

If we do not love our self, how can we accept that another loves us.

If we do not believe in our self, how can we accept that another believes in us.

If we do not trust our self, how can we accept that another trusts us.

If we are not true to our self, how can we accept that another is true to us.

If we are not honest with our self, how can we accept that another is being honest with us.

If we do not accept who we are as our self, how can we accept being loved for who we are by any other.

We must always begin with our self . . . The rest follows.

∞ ♥ ∞ ♥ ∞ ♥ ∞ ♥ ∞ ♥ ∞ ♥ ∞ ♥ ∞ ♥ ∞ ♥ ∞ ♥ ∞ ♥ ∞ ♥ ∞ ♥ ∞ ♥ ∞ ♥ ∞ ♥

Thank you Father for the beauty & events held within this day;
Thank you for the blessings sent my way.

As the sunlight kisses the water, its' warmth caresses my face;
My mind travels to another time & place;
The surface, it glistens & shines with light from above;
As always, I feel as if surrounded in love.

∞ ♥ ∞ ♥ ∞ ♥ ∞ ♥ ∞ ♥ ∞ ♥ ∞ ♥ ∞ ♥ ∞ ♥ ∞ ♥ ∞ ♥ ∞ ♥ ∞ ♥ ∞ ♥ ∞ ♥ ∞ ♥

There is a love that I hold for all that is in my life;
For the people, places & creatures of the air, water & earth;
Moments of time, finding joy & happiness replaces hardships & strife;
My thoughts set free, thereby, my imagination allowing new birth.

∞ ♥ ∞ ♥ ∞ ♥ ∞ ♥ ∞ ♥ ∞ ♥ ∞ ♥ ∞ ♥ ∞ ♥ ∞ ♥ ∞ ♥ ∞ ♥ ∞ ♥ ∞ ♥ ∞ ♥ ∞ ♥

There is a rhythm to life, the rhythm of love;
When in need of help, it comes from above;
There are those here also willing to lend a hand;
To pick us back up, staying to once more help us stand.

∞ ♥ ∞ ♥ ∞ ♥ ∞ ♥ ∞ ♥ ∞ ♥ ∞ ♥ ∞ ♥ ∞ ♥ ∞ ♥ ∞ ♥ ∞ ♥ ∞ ♥ ∞ ♥ ∞ ♥ ∞ ♥

We may not hear what we want to hear,
But we will know what we need to know;
A friend will forever hold you dear,
Unconditional love always willing to show.

∞ ♥ ∞ ♥ ∞ ♥ ∞ ♥ ∞ ♥ ∞ ♥ ∞ ♥ ∞ ♥ ∞ ♥ ∞ ♥ ∞ ♥ ∞ ♥ ∞ ♥ ∞ ♥ ∞ ♥ ∞ ♥

So much we have to say, so much we have to do;
Always grateful for the time I can spend with you;
Through the blessings we receive & the blessings we give;
It is truly a wonderful life we have chosen to live.

∞ ♥ ∞ ♥ ∞ ♥ ∞ ♥ ∞ ♥ ∞ ♥ ∞ ♥ ∞ ♥ ∞ ♥ ∞ ♥ ∞ ♥ ∞ ♥ ∞ ♥ ∞ ♥ ∞ ♥ ∞ ♥

In awe of so much from this world in which I live;

Cherishing the gifts I receive from the blessings you give;

Believing in miracles, happy endings & that love can conquer all;

Live life to the fullest, no regrets—go out & have a ball.

∞ ♥ ∞ ♥ ∞ ♥ ∞ ♥ ∞ ♥ ∞ ♥ ∞ ♥ ∞ ♥ ∞ ♥ ∞ ♥ ∞ ♥ ∞ ♥ ∞ ♥ ∞ ♥ ∞ ♥ ∞ ♥ ∞ ♥ ∞ ♥

As the sun rises each day, I am reminded of your love;

My life I have given to you, in selflessness I try to live my days;

Pleasures found simply enjoying life, like spending time under the Sun, Moon & Stars above;

Side by side you are with me & faithfully trusting you always.

∞ ♥ ∞ ♥ ∞ ♥ ∞ ♥ ∞ ♥ ∞ ♥ ∞ ♥ ∞ ♥ ∞ ♥ ∞ ♥ ∞ ♥ ∞ ♥ ∞ ♥ ∞ ♥ ∞ ♥ ∞ ♥ ∞ ♥ ∞ ♥

Feel the love held within my heart, use it to heal thine own;

Look into my eyes, see my soul, see me as I truly am, to you, it shall be shown.

∞ ♥ ∞ ♥ ∞ ♥ ∞ ♥ ∞ ♥ ∞ ♥ ∞ ♥ ∞ ♥ ∞ ♥ ∞ ♥ ∞ ♥ ∞ ♥ ∞ ♥ ∞ ♥ ∞ ♥ ∞ ♥ ∞ ♥ ∞ ♥

Life in its' simplest state can be so profound;

Taking in each moment, each treasure;

Through all of the senses, blessings abound;

Life lived in love . . . its' worth is beyond measure.

As we walk in this world, moving forward, we make our way;

Having the knowledge we are accountable for each of our own thoughts,

words & deeds every moment of every day;

To love yourself is "to thine own self be true";

Allowing you to accept & love all others in all you think, say & do;

I am who I am, for another I cannot be;

Take time to look into my heart, to look into my eyes then seeing my

soul you will truly see me;

Then make a choice to stay in my life or turn & walk away;

Knowing whatever path you choose, within my heart forever you will

stay.

The birds singing sweetly, their beautiful morning songs;
While rain drops gently fall to the earth where they belong;
The sun shining brightly, continuously through it all;
A whisper gently saying, come & play for a time—have a ball.

∞ ♥ ∞ ♥ ∞ ♥ ∞ ♥ ∞ ♥ ∞ ♥ ∞ ♥ ∞ ♥ ∞ ♥ ∞ ♥ ∞ ♥ ∞ ♥ ∞ ♥ ∞ ♥ ∞ ♥ ∞ ♥

Have you ever felt that you are alone in this world but something deep
within you tells you that you are never really alone;
Finding a contentment in life, living life all on your own;
Have you held a faith in something so great, others may think you are
insane;
But again from somewhere deep within, you know a truth you cannot
explain;
Have you ever known before hand how others would act or what they
would say;
Then experience it like a deja vu near or on the same day;
Somehow deep within knowing exactly how the words or actions will
come into play;
But knowing everything is ok.

∞ ♥ ∞ ♥ ∞ ♥ ∞ ♥ ∞ ♥ ∞ ♥ ∞ ♥ ∞ ♥ ∞ ♥ ∞ ♥ ∞ ♥ ∞ ♥ ∞ ♥ ∞ ♥ ∞ ♥ ∞ ♥

I seek & find all that I hold dear;

Dreams become reality when I can let go of the fear;

In each step, each choice, each breath, with life there is risk, so I take the chance;

Allowing my heart to sing as my soul leads my feet in life's beautiful dance.

Thoughts of one held dear;

Memories of laughter & good cheer;

In times of trouble or sadness, the one who was always there first;

A mother & a friend with enough love to quench every thirst;

Capable of lending a hand & at the same time setting things straight;

A mothers' love only God can create.

I believe in miracles, I have Faith all my needs shall be met;

I believe my Father has a plan for me, although I may not see it yet.

All in life is exactly as it is meant to be;

Whether it is for you or for me;

Free-will we are given for there are choices we must make;

Determining the difference on which path in life we take;

Accountable & responsible for each step, each thought, each word along the way;

Awareness of this makes it easy to be respectful of all life, all others each & every day

One moment in time can make such a difference in life.

You are loved by those near, you are loved from afar;

You are loved by those who are in heaven with the Angels amongst the stars;

You are loved always, it does not matter we are not side by side;

Look to the heavens, let love & light be your guide.

∞ ♥ ∞ ♥ ∞ ♥ ∞ ♥ ∞ ♥ ∞ ♥ ∞ ♥ ∞ ♥ ∞ ♥ ∞ ♥ ∞ ♥ ∞ ♥ ∞ ♥ ∞ ♥ ∞ ♥ ∞ ♥ ∞ ♥

Life I find holds many joys & many sorrows;

Endlessly filling my yesterdays, todays & tomorrows;

I have to admit, I feel that the happiness outweighs the pain;

But one without the other there would be no lesson to gain.

As the birds chirp & the spiders' web glistens in the early morning sun;

A joy for life fills my heart for this new day begun.

∞ ♥ ∞ ♥ ∞ ♥ ∞ ♥ ∞ ♥ ∞ ♥ ∞ ♥ ∞ ♥ ∞ ♥ ∞ ♥ ∞ ♥ ∞ ♥ ∞ ♥ ∞ ♥ ∞ ♥ ∞ ♥ ∞ ♥

With Faith in my heart I will let my heart lead my way;

With Faith in my heart my love for life continues to grow each day;

With Faith in my heart I will live life without fear;

With Faith in my heart I hold my adventures in life dear;

With Faith in my heart all blessings in life I will see;

With Faith in my heart I will share who I am, be exactly who my Father created me to be.

∞ ♥ ∞ ♥ ∞ ♥ ∞ ♥ ∞ ♥ ∞ ♥ ∞ ♥ ∞ ♥ ∞ ♥ ∞ ♥ ∞ ♥ ∞ ♥ ∞ ♥ ∞ ♥ ∞ ♥ ∞ ♥ ∞ ♥

A life filled with love, happiness & joy, is the path I choose;
I have everything to gain & nothing to lose;
So I brighten someone else's day with smiles & laughter I have to share;
Showing a stranger or a friend, another does care.

∞ ♥ ∞ ♥ ∞ ♥ ∞ ♥ ∞ ♥ ∞ ♥ ∞ ♥ ∞ ♥ ∞ ♥ ∞ ♥ ∞ ♥ ∞ ♥ ∞ ♥ ∞ ♥ ∞ ♥ ∞ ♥

The world around me, has changed before my eyes;
Everything new, the land, the trees & even the skies;
Amazed by nature, in awe of the beauty I have found;
Seeing every need for every creature taken care of through our Fathers'
generosity & love—Blessings Abound.

∞ ♥ ∞ ♥ ∞ ♥ ∞ ♥ ∞ ♥ ∞ ♥ ∞ ♥ ∞ ♥ ∞ ♥ ∞ ♥ ∞ ♥ ∞ ♥ ∞ ♥ ∞ ♥ ∞ ♥ ∞ ♥

When wanting to understand another, we must first look within &
understand, even accept ones' self—the shadows & the light;
It has been taught by many masters throughout the centuries, when
we see or experience a trait of another that we dislike, it is generally
a reflection of that part of ourselves that we need to confront within
ourselves—therefore we have the tools to take that which is wrong &
making it right . . .

∞ ♥ ∞ ♥ ∞ ♥ ∞ ♥ ∞ ♥ ∞ ♥ ∞ ♥ ∞ ♥ ∞ ♥ ∞ ♥ ∞ ♥ ∞ ♥ ∞ ♥ ∞ ♥ ∞ ♥ ∞ ♥

I dream many dreams, letting my imagination run wild;

The visions I see are like those seen through the eyes of a child;

Everything vibrant, full of life, everything new;

Yet the dreams I have are not for me alone, they are also for you.

In silence & solitude I begin my day;

Pondering life's events that have come my way;

Each event strengthening, tempering my mind, body & soul, like that of a warriors' blade;

To continue my lifes' quest with courage each step is made;

With love & compassion I will live yet for that which I believe in I will firmly stand;

Even as new events continue to change me—As I am continually molded by the

Potters' Hands.

A calmness in the air after the storms of yesterday;

A stillness within nature for a while has come to stay;

A Hawk soars above me, its' wings spread wide;

Its' magnificence & beauty naturally seen, for that, it seems, it cannot hide.

Taking time to relax, I sit daydreaming, watching the clouds casually roll by;

Two Eagles appear soaring, seemingly without a care in the southern sky;

As I watch them my spirit soars as well;

Then a thought as if a gentle whisper says, "you have a story to tell";

As they disappear from my sight flying farther south;

To my amazement a Hawk & its' mate appear over me, with one another their flight completely in sync, "How beautiful", were the words that came out of my mouth.

Friend . . .

To me, a friend will stand by your side through good times & bad;

A friend will lend an ear to hear all about what's going on whether you are happy or sad;

A friend will pick you up at those times in life when you fall;

A friend will tell you the truth regardless of the outcome of it all;

A friend has the courage to say the things you need to hear, even if there is a chance you will turn & walk away;

A friend will love you for your faults as well as your talents & remain a friend day after day.

∞ ♥ ∞ ♥ ∞ ♥ ∞ ♥ ∞ ♥ ∞ ♥ ∞ ♥ ∞ ♥ ∞ ♥ ∞ ♥ ∞ ♥ ∞ ♥ ∞ ♥ ∞ ♥ ∞ ♥ ∞ ♥ ∞ ♥

A respect for all in life needs to be held within the heart;
Beginning with oneself is the best place to start.

Up today not once but twice;
Sleep it seems is what I sacrifice;
First, it was the alarm that sent me on my way;
Second, my dog got in my face, saying, "come on, get up, I want to play."
Needed some lab work—under a doctor's care;
She seems to think I live a normal life, having plenty of time & blood
to spare.

If you follow your heart it will guide the way;
Leading you on the path in life you are meant to stay;
With faith you can open eyes, open hearts & open doors;
Miracles of life along your travels among valleys, mountains & distant
shores.

As I sit on the deck with a cup of morning brew;

This day, I have the sun & the moon both within my view;

A cool gentle morning breeze blows back my hair;

And birds sing their greeting while flying in the air;

For me, for a while, time stands still, noticing only my heart beating within my chest;

Feelings of peace, love & a balance within—this I have to say, it is the time I like best.

Masters of our own destiny, creators of our own fate;

Always our choice, either take a chance on life or sit around & wait.

∞ ♥ ∞ ♥ ∞ ♥ ∞ ♥ ∞ ♥ ∞ ♥ ∞ ♥ ∞ ♥ ∞ ♥ ∞ ♥ ∞ ♥ ∞ ♥ ∞ ♥ ∞ ♥ ∞ ♥

To give of yourself freely, unconditionally, without any strings attached, without any expectation of a return;

Is a gift given in love, making a difference in life—yours as well as others—each encounter carrying a lesson to learn.

∞ ♥ ∞ ♥ ∞ ♥ ∞ ♥ ∞ ♥ ∞ ♥ ∞ ♥ ∞ ♥ ∞ ♥ ∞ ♥ ∞ ♥ ∞ ♥ ∞ ♥ ∞ ♥ ∞ ♥

Do not let fear of rejection hinder your heart;

Live life with a passion from beginning to end;

Love with all that you have—each new day we have a brand new start;

Let the fires burning within your soul shine, as you may be for someone a much needed light, be they a stranger or a friend.

∞ ♥ ∞ ♥ ∞ ♥ ∞ ♥ ∞ ♥ ∞ ♥ ∞ ♥ ∞ ♥ ∞ ♥ ∞ ♥ ∞ ♥ ∞ ♥ ∞ ♥ ∞ ♥ ∞ ♥ ∞ ♥ ∞ ♥

Yesterday the winds of change blew strong;

Today peace & serenity have come along;

Blessed with love & protection each & every day;

Allowing the light within to shine even in the darkest of hours, it will illuminate & guide the way.

∞ ♥ ∞ ♥ ∞ ♥ ∞ ♥ ∞ ♥ ∞ ♥ ∞ ♥ ∞ ♥ ∞ ♥ ∞ ♥ ∞ ♥ ∞ ♥ ∞ ♥ ∞ ♥ ∞ ♥ ∞ ♥ ∞ ♥

I cannot help but giggle at the sight that I see;

A robin & a flicker on the same branch of a tree;

One right side up, the other upside down;

Showing me even in a topsy-turvy world, through faith, what we seek can be found.

∞ ♥ ∞ ♥ ∞ ♥ ∞ ♥ ∞ ♥ ∞ ♥ ∞ ♥ ∞ ♥ ∞ ♥ ∞ ♥ ∞ ♥ ∞ ♥ ∞ ♥ ∞ ♥ ∞ ♥ ∞ ♥ ∞ ♥

As clouds of grey gently shed water for the earth;
With the backdrop of the grey, everything is so vibrant & green, among the grass & trees;
Changes creating a beauty through growth & new birth;
I love the scent of rain, drifting on a gentle breeze.

∞ ♥ ∞ ♥ ∞ ♥ ∞ ♥ ∞ ♥ ∞ ♥ ∞ ♥ ∞ ♥ ∞ ♥ ∞ ♥ ∞ ♥ ∞ ♥ ∞ ♥ ∞ ♥ ∞ ♥ ∞ ♥

The paths some walk, I do not think I will ever understand;
Sometimes it is easy to see when you are outside looking in;
When we stumble & fall, we hope someone who cares will lend a hand;
Without judgment of choices as each is meant to walk their own path—so treating others as you wish to be treated is a good place to begin.

∞ ♥ ∞ ♥ ∞ ♥ ∞ ♥ ∞ ♥ ∞ ♥ ∞ ♥ ∞ ♥ ∞ ♥ ∞ ♥ ∞ ♥ ∞ ♥ ∞ ♥ ∞ ♥ ∞ ♥ ∞ ♥

Winged creatures or creations, I am drawn to, I adore;
Whether Angels or Eagles or Dragons of yore;
I find myself surrounded by all of the above;
With their guidance & protection I am surrounded by love.

∞ ♥ ∞ ♥ ∞ ♥ ∞ ♥ ∞ ♥ ∞ ♥ ∞ ♥ ∞ ♥ ∞ ♥ ∞ ♥ ∞ ♥ ∞ ♥ ∞ ♥ ∞ ♥ ∞ ♥ ∞ ♥

Thank you Father for the beautiful day;
Thank you for all the sunshine & blue skies you sent my way;
Thank you for every blessing large & small;
Thank you with all of my heart, I love them all.

There is so much belonging to this world, so much to see;
So many things to be taught, allowing many ways of growth for you & me;
With an open heart, an open mind the path will be made clear to thee.

∞ ♥ ∞ ♥ ∞ ♥ ∞ ♥ ∞ ♥ ∞ ♥ ∞ ♥ ∞ ♥ ∞ ♥ ∞ ♥ ∞ ♥ ∞ ♥ ∞ ♥ ∞ ♥ ∞ ♥ ∞ ♥

Have you ever felt as an outcast from the world around you? Yet having an innate sense of knowing you are exactly right where you belong. Alone, yet never really alone, as the world gently moves along.

∞ ♥ ∞ ♥ ∞ ♥ ∞ ♥ ∞ ♥ ∞ ♥ ∞ ♥ ∞ ♥ ∞ ♥ ∞ ♥ ∞ ♥ ∞ ♥ ∞ ♥ ∞ ♥ ∞ ♥ ∞ ♥

The rain has come yet another day;
Turning skies from blue to grey;
Leaving the colors of a rainbow behind;
Treasures within nature for me to find.

∞ ♥ ∞ ♥ ∞ ♥ ∞ ♥ ∞ ♥ ∞ ♥ ∞ ♥ ∞ ♥ ∞ ♥ ∞ ♥ ∞ ♥ ∞ ♥ ∞ ♥ ∞ ♥ ∞ ♥ ∞ ♥ ∞ ♥

During our life people will come, people will go;
Some allowing their heart & soul for you to know;
Some may shine brightly, others may seem a little dark;
Nobody said life would be a walk in the park;
So take each moment, make it worth while;
Taking time to love & share a smile.

∞ ♥ ∞ ♥ ∞ ♥ ∞ ♥ ∞ ♥ ∞ ♥ ∞ ♥ ∞ ♥ ∞ ♥ ∞ ♥ ∞ ♥ ∞ ♥ ∞ ♥ ∞ ♥ ∞ ♥ ∞ ♥ ∞ ♥

It is the beauty I find in the simplest of things;
A night sky filled with stars or the morning sun shining bright, as the
birds sing;
Wild flowers dancing in the breeze;
Mother Nature whispering softly through the leaves of the trees;
Light glistening upon the water, as the river slowly meanders by;
Grateful to be able to take it all in & feeling 'Blessed am I'.

195

Warmth & sunshine has come this way;
Everything within me says, "go out & play";
As I look around, there is much work to be done;
So, I will do what is needed & have some fun.

Laughter & memories filled my night;
Sharing with a friend made it all feel right;
So many events in my life have helped mold the woman I see;
I can truly say, I love being ME ☺

A hand reaching out, giving a soft, gentle touch;
The simplest of gestures can mean so much.

∞ ♥ ∞ ♥ ∞ ♥ ∞ ♥ ∞ ♥ ∞ ♥ ∞ ♥ ∞ ♥ ∞ ♥ ∞ ♥ ∞ ♥ ∞ ♥ ∞ ♥ ∞ ♥ ∞ ♥ ∞ ♥

My mind it travels to so many people, so many faces;
Instantly I feel I am in a thousand different places;
I travel near, I travel far, with wings of love I am taken there;
It is my mind, heart & soul that allows me to travel anywhere.

∞ ♥ ∞ ♥ ∞ ♥ ∞ ♥ ∞ ♥ ∞ ♥ ∞ ♥ ∞ ♥ ∞ ♥ ∞ ♥ ∞ ♥ ∞ ♥ ∞ ♥ ∞ ♥ ∞ ♥ ∞ ♥

Father, Angels, Masters above;
I thank you for surrounding me with unconditional love;
It is you that fills my mind, heart & soul;
Allowing the love within me, given to all life to flow.

∞ ♥ ∞ ♥ ∞ ♥ ∞ ♥ ∞ ♥ ∞ ♥ ∞ ♥ ∞ ♥ ∞ ♥ ∞ ♥ ∞ ♥ ∞ ♥ ∞ ♥ ∞ ♥ ∞ ♥ ∞ ♥

There are events in life, some beyond our control;
Events, if allowed, that can take a toll;
It is all in how we perceive the events that come our way;
Making a difference in how we learn, how we grow, every moment,
every day.

∞ ♥ ∞ ♥ ∞ ♥ ∞ ♥ ∞ ♥ ∞ ♥ ∞ ♥ ∞ ♥ ∞ ♥ ∞ ♥ ∞ ♥ ∞ ♥ ∞ ♥ ∞ ♥ ∞ ♥ ∞ ♥

With Faith, I awake to a bright new day;

Knowing my needs are met while on my path I stay;

My Fathers' Will, I pray shall be done, for He knows best;

Knowing I am surrounded in love as I continue my quest.

Take a look deep within, you shall find our Fathers' Light;

Through the magic of love it still burns strong, it still burns bright;

Allow your heart to guide your way, every step you take;

Here His words—"I AM with you now, I AM with you always. This is a wow I shall not break."

"Take my hand little one, walk by my side."

"For the love I hold for you I cannot hide."

I feel so tired, yet I cannot sleep;

Sometimes so exhausted all I can do is weep;

Yet a Faith through the courage of my heart, I keep.

∞ ♥ ∞ ♥ ∞ ♥ ∞ ♥ ∞ ♥ ∞ ♥ ∞ ♥ ∞ ♥ ∞ ♥ ∞ ♥ ∞ ♥ ∞ ♥ ∞ ♥ ∞ ♥ ∞ ♥ ∞ ♥

The first thing this morning as I stood by my door, drinking in the world that surrounds me;

A greeting from a humming bird, whom showed no fear, amazed me;

He flew right up to me & hovered near, so close to my face, I could see every detail of his tiny feathers—greens & reds & whites;

A blessing from nature, I have no doubt, a reminder of beauty, joy, freedom, fearlessness & so much more;

There is much to this world that touches my heart;

I am grateful for the blessings within my life as each day I once again start.

Today is but a dream of my yesterday;

Tomorrow is my dream of today.

∞ ♥ ∞ ♥ ∞ ♥ ∞ ♥ ∞ ♥ ∞ ♥ ∞ ♥ ∞ ♥ ∞ ♥ ∞ ♥ ∞ ♥ ∞ ♥ ∞ ♥ ∞ ♥ ∞ ♥ ∞ ♥

Have you ever had a phrase just stick in your head;

From the very first moment you woke up in bed;

Today this is the phrase that has come my way;

"Smile & Have A Nice Day!"

∞ ♥ ∞ ♥ ∞ ♥ ∞ ♥ ∞ ♥ ∞ ♥ ∞ ♥ ∞ ♥ ∞ ♥ ∞ ♥ ∞ ♥ ∞ ♥ ∞ ♥ ∞ ♥ ∞ ♥ ∞ ♥

Thank you Father for such a beautiful day;
For always caring for those near & far away.

The moon & stars guide me by night;
The sun blesses me throughout the day with its' light;
It matters not if the skies are darkened & grey;
For it is always the light that guides my way.

Blessing upon blessing is what I see;
Not just for myself but for everyone around me;
Life is only as good as we allow it to be;
The blessings are there just waiting for you to see;
Believe With All Your Heart—Blessed Be.

Waves of love are sent through the air;

To all I have ever known, to all for whom I care;

If you feel a gentle touch, warm embrace;

As it touches your heart—a smile shall find its place;

Like ripples, never ending, it travels all the heavens & earth;

Allowing the fire within to burn strong & bright, the gift given through birth.

∞ ♥ ∞ ♥ ∞ ♥ ∞ ♥ ∞ ♥ ∞ ♥ ∞ ♥ ∞ ♥ ∞ ♥ ∞ ♥ ∞ ♥ ∞ ♥ ∞ ♥ ∞ ♥ ∞ ♥ ∞ ♥ ∞ ♥

My mind & body yearn for your touch;

The desire is from deep within, where the longing is such;

Touch me, feel me, for it is pleasure I seek;

Pleasures between a man & woman are that which I speak.

∞ ♥ ∞ ♥ ∞ ♥ ∞ ♥ ∞ ♥ ∞ ♥ ∞ ♥ ∞ ♥ ∞ ♥ ∞ ♥ ∞ ♥ ∞ ♥ ∞ ♥ ∞ ♥ ∞ ♥ ∞ ♥ ∞ ♥

Dreams becoming real;

Life taking my breath away;

It is all of my heart with which I love & feel;

Enjoying each moment, each day.

∞ ♥ ∞ ♥ ∞ ♥ ∞ ♥ ∞ ♥ ∞ ♥ ∞ ♥ ∞ ♥ ∞ ♥ ∞ ♥ ∞ ♥ ∞ ♥ ∞ ♥ ∞ ♥ ∞ ♥ ∞ ♥ ∞ ♥

Owls by night, Hawks by day;
Grateful for this life in every way.

A bright new day has begun;
I am up to greet the sun;
As I listen to birds sing their morning songs;
I understand with nature I am right where I belong;
Grateful for all, whether, Eagles, Turkeys, Humming birds, Butterflies
or Dragonflies;
Excited for the adventures in this day that ahead of me lies.

Blessed be as the day has begun;
For the weaver of Magic, whom has a silver tongue;
Through the words that you sent, paradise came to me;
Both, now fantasy & dreams I hope my reality to be;
For within me now are desires & treasures untold;
It is you who holds the key to unlock, to experience them unfold.

∞ ♥ ∞ ♥ ∞ ♥ ∞ ♥ ∞ ♥ ∞ ♥ ∞ ♥ ∞ ♥ ∞ ♥ ∞ ♥ ∞ ♥ ∞ ♥ ∞ ♥ ∞ ♥ ∞ ♥ ∞ ♥

Thank you Father for all blessings this day;
For the beauty I see & feel in every way;
Thank you for meeting all of my needs allowing to come what may;
For always in my mind, heart & soul you shall stay.

∞ ♥ ∞ ♥ ∞ ♥ ∞ ♥ ∞ ♥ ∞ ♥ ∞ ♥ ∞ ♥ ∞ ♥ ∞ ♥ ∞ ♥ ∞ ♥ ∞ ♥ ∞ ♥ ∞ ♥ ∞ ♥

Ahh, the timeless beauty life does hold;
Allowing pictures to be painted, so vibrant & bold.

∞ ♥ ∞ ♥ ∞ ♥ ∞ ♥ ∞ ♥ ∞ ♥ ∞ ♥ ∞ ♥ ∞ ♥ ∞ ♥ ∞ ♥ ∞ ♥ ∞ ♥ ∞ ♥ ∞ ♥ ∞ ♥

Treasures of the heart, treasures of the mind;
Treasures of the soul, await for you to find;
Treasures of the earth, treasures in heaven above;
Treasures greatest of all, to me, are those of love.

∞ ♥ ∞ ♥ ∞ ♥ ∞ ♥ ∞ ♥ ∞ ♥ ∞ ♥ ∞ ♥ ∞ ♥ ∞ ♥ ∞ ♥ ∞ ♥ ∞ ♥ ∞ ♥ ∞ ♥ ∞ ♥

A service to God, a service to man;

A day to remember all who have served this land;

Lives given by choice so freedom remains at hand;

A sacrifice made of years & perhaps personal plans;

Thank you for loving so many, to give so much of yourself while in harms way have had to stand.

A life of service to God, to man;

Giving part or all of your life seemingly part of the plan;

Thank you to those who have served & protected through the years, now & so long ago.

To anyone who has served in the military or law enforcement, currently or in the past;

Thank you for caring enough, that you have given so much & asking so little in return;

You, whether here on earth or in heaven above;

Have my heartfelt gratitude & love.

One so distant, though they are near;
One so near, though they are distant, overcoming fear.

∞ ♥ ∞ ♥ ∞ ♥ ∞ ♥ ∞ ♥ ∞ ♥ ∞ ♥ ∞ ♥ ∞ ♥ ∞ ♥ ∞ ♥ ∞ ♥ ∞ ♥ ∞ ♥ ∞ ♥ ∞ ♥

Blessed be this day, for each & everyone;
Surrounded with love & light as brilliant as the sun;
The light of love is strong within us & we cannot conceal;
It opens our hearts & eyes to all that love does reveal;
Our soul knowing the truth as love lights the way;
Blessed be, each & everyone, forever & a day.

∞ ♥ ∞ ♥ ∞ ♥ ∞ ♥ ∞ ♥ ∞ ♥ ∞ ♥ ∞ ♥ ∞ ♥ ∞ ♥ ∞ ♥ ∞ ♥ ∞ ♥ ∞ ♥ ∞ ♥ ∞ ♥

I freely receive the love as it is given, I freely give the love that is my own;
Allowing good within life, understanding we reap that which we have sown.

∞ ♥ ∞ ♥ ∞ ♥ ∞ ♥ ∞ ♥ ∞ ♥ ∞ ♥ ∞ ♥ ∞ ♥ ∞ ♥ ∞ ♥ ∞ ♥ ∞ ♥ ∞ ♥ ∞ ♥ ∞ ♥

The choice is yours if you stay or you depart;

The choice is yours if you listen to others or listen to your heart;

The choice is yours because you are free;

The choice is yours because of the divine gift given to you & me;

The choice is yours as I choose to love you unconditionally;

The choice is yours to love me as I am or let me be.

When a soul does leave this earthly plane;

The love created shall forever remain;

A sadness is felt by those who are left behind it is true;

May all feel the comfort of love that is constantly surrounding you.

Wild flowers are like Gods' personal artwork of this world;

Amazed by their own kind of magic as each becomes unfurled;

So much beauty, each unique & wonderful in its' own way;

Take time to "smell the roses" & have a fantastic day.

∞ ♥ ∞ ♥ ∞ ♥ ∞ ♥ ∞ ♥ ∞ ♥ ∞ ♥ ∞ ♥ ∞ ♥ ∞ ♥ ∞ ♥ ∞ ♥ ∞ ♥ ∞ ♥ ∞ ♥ ∞ ♥

What once was lost shall again be found;
Blessings for you from the universe abound.

∞ ♥ ∞ ♥ ∞ ♥ ∞ ♥ ∞ ♥ ∞ ♥ ∞ ♥ ∞ ♥ ∞ ♥ ∞ ♥ ∞ ♥ ∞ ♥ ∞ ♥ ∞ ♥ ∞ ♥ ∞ ♥ ∞ ♥

I place you in our Fathers' tender loving care;
Surrounded by His love, light & truth, always knowing you are
protected there;
He watches over you throughout the day & night;
Illuminating the shadows with His pure radiating white light.

∞ ♥ ∞ ♥ ∞ ♥ ∞ ♥ ∞ ♥ ∞ ♥ ∞ ♥ ∞ ♥ ∞ ♥ ∞ ♥ ∞ ♥ ∞ ♥ ∞ ♥ ∞ ♥ ∞ ♥ ∞ ♥ ∞ ♥

Life goes on day to day;
Life goes on allowing let come what may;
Living without expectations of another whether a friendship or love;
Living without judgment or deception as guided from above;
Life goes on having no regrets, no fears;
Life goes on leaving beauty to look back on over the years.

∞ ♥ ∞ ♥ ∞ ♥ ∞ ♥ ∞ ♥ ∞ ♥ ∞ ♥ ∞ ♥ ∞ ♥ ∞ ♥ ∞ ♥ ∞ ♥ ∞ ♥ ∞ ♥ ∞ ♥ ∞ ♥

As the flower bends each morning in search of the light of the sun;
I too reach out searching for my Fathers' light as each of my days is begun.

My mind, it travels both near & far;
With the Faith of a child, my heart & soul still wish upon a star;
Through the dreams I have, the voices are clear;
My mind whispering messages in my subconscious' ear.

A field of green lays before my eyes;
Above me the sun & crescent moon appear in the clear blue skies;
A day of blessings has come once more;
Loving life & the adventures it holds for me to explore.
Thank you Father for all of the blessings you bring;
For my soul that has knowledge of love & a heart with which to sing;
For my mind that acknowledges You & all of the blessings you bring.

A prayer is held within the depths of my soul;

A prayer that you are aware of love held for you, a love so much greater than you know;

A love so unconditional that is with you wherever you go;

A love between a mother and child, no matter how near or far, continues to grow.

∞ ♥ ∞ ♥ ∞ ♥ ∞ ♥ ∞ ♥ ∞ ♥ ∞ ♥ ∞ ♥ ∞ ♥ ∞ ♥ ∞ ♥ ∞ ♥ ∞ ♥ ∞ ♥ ∞ ♥ ∞ ♥

For Tyler

Blessed be little one, as this is your celebration day;

Who could have known, an Angel would come 7 years ago today;

Blessed be little one as you touch so many with your love & light;

I am grateful for you, as you make the world happy & bright

Happy Birthday Tyler Alexa Love Always, Grandma Rita

∞ ♥ ∞ ♥ ∞ ♥ ∞ ♥ ∞ ♥ ∞ ♥ ∞ ♥ ∞ ♥ ∞ ♥ ∞ ♥ ∞ ♥ ∞ ♥ ∞ ♥ ∞ ♥ ∞ ♥ ∞ ♥

I would give you the world, but it is not mine to give;
I would give you the sun & moon, but how would the world then live;
I give you all I can but is it ever enough . . .
I give you my love for it is truly the only gift I have to give.

The Universe is the keeper of many truths untold;
As we seek the knowledge shall unfold;
The answers to questions await from days of old;
Find the treasure before you with the key you hold.

∞ ♥ ∞ ♥ ∞ ♥ ∞ ♥ ∞ ♥ ∞ ♥ ∞ ♥ ∞ ♥ ∞ ♥ ∞ ♥ ∞ ♥ ∞ ♥ ∞ ♥ ∞ ♥ ∞ ♥ ∞ ♥ ∞ ♥

There is a crystalline light, how it dances chasing all shadows away;
Its light brighter than the sun, bringing happiness & love, lasting forever & a day.
The shadows did fight, twisting & turning in the night;
Through the power of love of many into one, there remains love & protection in the illuminating light.

∞ ♥ ∞ ♥ ∞ ♥ ∞ ♥ ∞ ♥ ∞ ♥ ∞ ♥ ∞ ♥ ∞ ♥ ∞ ♥ ∞ ♥ ∞ ♥ ∞ ♥ ∞ ♥ ∞ ♥ ∞ ♥ ∞ ♥

There may be many things in life we do not completely understand;

My thoughts just traveled to a photo of a mother & child walking on a beach;

The two taking in the beauty around them, while walking hand in hand;

All the while, the child trusting, the mother knowing through love she would always protect her while she also had many lessons to teach.

∞ ♥ ∞ ♥ ∞ ♥ ∞ ♥ ∞ ♥ ∞ ♥ ∞ ♥ ∞ ♥ ∞ ♥ ∞ ♥ ∞ ♥ ∞ ♥ ∞ ♥ ∞ ♥ ∞ ♥ ∞ ♥

"Love transcends death, people we love touch our lives, even after they are gone."

∞ ♥ ∞ ♥ ∞ ♥ ∞ ♥ ∞ ♥ ∞ ♥ ∞ ♥ ∞ ♥ ∞ ♥ ∞ ♥ ∞ ♥ ∞ ♥ ∞ ♥ ∞ ♥ ∞ ♥ ∞ ♥

Life is a gift, each one precious & rare;

Life is too short for misery & despair;

Share life with others, as well as a smile;

Finding happiness & joys, contentment & love, enjoying life all the while.

∞ ♥ ∞ ♥ ∞ ♥ ∞ ♥ ∞ ♥ ∞ ♥ ∞ ♥ ∞ ♥ ∞ ♥ ∞ ♥ ∞ ♥ ∞ ♥ ∞ ♥ ∞ ♥ ∞ ♥ ∞ ♥

If we hold no expectations of another's thoughts, actions or emotions—we shall have no disappointments;
If we hold our self accountable & responsible for our own thoughts, actions & emotions—we shall have contentment.

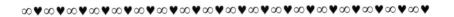

Without expectations we can experience no disappointment;
With gratitude we can experience happiness & joy.

Life is grandest in the simplest of ways;
Drink in the beauty that surrounds you all of your days.

"Life is your cup—Drink it up"

Through the purest of love held within my heart & the fires' light of my soul;

I have attained balance between my body & spirit;

Through many changes in life—remaining loyal to those I love—even through heartaches & pain, there has always been happiness & joys;

Not an easy journey to make, yet eternally grateful for making it & being allowed to continually grow.

∞ ♥ ∞ ♥ ∞ ♥ ∞ ♥ ∞ ♥ ∞ ♥ ∞ ♥ ∞ ♥ ∞ ♥ ∞ ♥ ∞ ♥ ∞ ♥ ∞ ♥ ∞ ♥ ∞ ♥ ∞ ♥ ∞ ♥

There is so much beauty of this world & beyond that awaits for you to see;

Open your eyes & follow your heart when it gently whispers . . ."come I shall lead the way, follow me."

∞ ♥ ∞ ♥ ∞ ♥ ∞ ♥ ∞ ♥ ∞ ♥ ∞ ♥ ∞ ♥ ∞ ♥ ∞ ♥ ∞ ♥ ∞ ♥ ∞ ♥ ∞ ♥ ∞ ♥ ∞ ♥ ∞ ♥

Dreams tell a story of the subconscious mind;

Desires & fears appearing to show secrets for you to find;

Hidden wisdom allows you to see some of darkness, some that is kind;

Dreams reveal much through our subconscious mind.

∞ ♥ ∞ ♥ ∞ ♥ ∞ ♥ ∞ ♥ ∞ ♥ ∞ ♥ ∞ ♥ ∞ ♥ ∞ ♥ ∞ ♥ ∞ ♥ ∞ ♥ ∞ ♥ ∞ ♥ ∞ ♥ ∞ ♥

Blessed be on this glorious day;

Our morning star has come out to play;

As the robins feed & butterflies dance;

I am grateful for all I see in a moments glance;

Humming birds that stop right in front of me;

Gentle reminders in all seasons, there are many blessings to see.

∞ ♥ ∞ ♥ ∞ ♥ ∞ ♥ ∞ ♥ ∞ ♥ ∞ ♥ ∞ ♥ ∞ ♥ ∞ ♥ ∞ ♥ ∞ ♥ ∞ ♥ ∞ ♥ ∞ ♥ ∞ ♥ ∞ ♥

Morning birds sing their songs as the wind carries it through the trees;

Winds are whispering a song of their own as the butterflies dance in the breeze;

Within my head music does play;

Also singing, "It's gonna be a bright, bright, bright sunshiny day."

∞ ♥ ∞ ♥ ∞ ♥ ∞ ♥ ∞ ♥ ∞ ♥ ∞ ♥ ∞ ♥ ∞ ♥ ∞ ♥ ∞ ♥ ∞ ♥ ∞ ♥ ∞ ♥ ∞ ♥ ∞ ♥

My prayers for you are that you are kept safe & sound;

After the storms, joys like rainbows are found;

That you find the strength as needed within you;

To tackle any storms & at the end like a rainbow come shining through.

My life I place in your trusting hands;
With faith I trust you, my destiny as it stands;
Where you lead me, I will follow;
For without you in my life, I am empty & hollow.

∞ ♥ ∞ ♥ ∞ ♥ ∞ ♥ ∞ ♥ ∞ ♥ ∞ ♥ ∞ ♥ ∞ ♥ ∞ ♥ ∞ ♥ ∞ ♥ ∞ ♥ ∞ ♥ ∞ ♥ ∞ ♥ ∞ ♥

Fate & destination;
Live life without hesitations;
Hold no expectations;
Need no explanations;
Love life's celebrations.

∞ ♥ ∞ ♥ ∞ ♥ ∞ ♥ ∞ ♥ ∞ ♥ ∞ ♥ ∞ ♥ ∞ ♥ ∞ ♥ ∞ ♥ ∞ ♥ ∞ ♥ ∞ ♥ ∞ ♥ ∞ ♥ ∞ ♥

Summers flowers in bloom under a clear blue sky;
A love filled heart, how grateful am I;
Having coffee on the deck as I sit with a friend;
There is no better way for part of my day to spend;
Prayers filled with love are heaven sent for you;
May all of your prayers be answered & your dreams come true.

∞ ♥ ∞ ♥ ∞ ♥ ∞ ♥ ∞ ♥ ∞ ♥ ∞ ♥ ∞ ♥ ∞ ♥ ∞ ♥ ∞ ♥ ∞ ♥ ∞ ♥ ∞ ♥ ∞ ♥ ∞ ♥ ∞ ♥

There is only one man in this world, he holds the key to my heart;
I pray when we meet, from one another, we never shall part;
I await in anticipation of his arrival, before a mid summers day;
Having requested the Sun, Moon & Stars to guide him to me, I pray.

One heart, mind, body, soul

With faith I believe in my Fate & Destiny;
I believe all shall be exactly as it is meant to be;
No accidents or coincidences in this life of mine;
All is part of the perfect plan divine.

Father, within your loving hands I have placed my heart;

In seeking true love that is the best place for me to start;

For I have faith you will guide me to the man I am to love;

Who will love me equally, as he is also guided from above;

Two shall be one heart, mind, body & soul;

As we are to fulfill our destiny, our ultimate goal.

∞ ♥ ∞ ♥ ∞ ♥ ∞ ♥ ∞ ♥ ∞ ♥ ∞ ♥ ∞ ♥ ∞ ♥ ∞ ♥ ∞ ♥ ∞ ♥ ∞ ♥ ∞ ♥ ∞ ♥ ∞ ♥ ∞ ♥

My hearts desire is to have you by my side;

I vow to share all of me for I have nothing to hide;

To accept you for exactly who you are always;

Together a life filled with love all of my days.

∞ ♥ ∞ ♥ ∞ ♥ ∞ ♥ ∞ ♥ ∞ ♥ ∞ ♥ ∞ ♥ ∞ ♥ ∞ ♥ ∞ ♥ ∞ ♥ ∞ ♥ ∞ ♥ ∞ ♥ ∞ ♥ ∞ ♥

There is a calm, a peace, a gentleness in the air;

The world momentarily serene with beauty to share;

My thoughts flooded with memories of long ago as well as my yesterday;

Smiles, from my heart, my soul realizing the many blessings filling all of my days.

∞ ♥ ∞ ♥ ∞ ♥ ∞ ♥ ∞ ♥ ∞ ♥ ∞ ♥ ∞ ♥ ∞ ♥ ∞ ♥ ∞ ♥ ∞ ♥ ∞ ♥ ∞ ♥ ∞ ♥ ∞ ♥ ∞ ♥

Awakened by a call at 5:30 am this morning allowed me to witness the start of a beautiful new day;

Tiniest of droplets, clinging to spiders' weavings made in the night, glistening as if by magic in some way;

Seeing the master at work of all of creation through dense fog, watching the sun rise, a brilliant white ball of light;

And the gift of a rose given unexpectedly, from a new planting not long ago, so lovely, its' color so bright;

So many blessings in life & to me they are blessings indeed;

We may not always have everything we want, but we do have everything we need.

There is so much in life we create with our own hands;

As a master weaver, one moment after another, placed side by side;

Each choice we make determining the color of each strand;

A tapestry of life revealing all, for there is nothing we may hide;

Moment by moment, choice by choice, thread by thread, we create with our own hands.

The beauty unfolds right before my eyes;
Nature reveals its' own disguise;
This life is mine, a loving cup;
My cup runneth over, although I continually drink it up.

∞ ♥ ∞ ♥ ∞ ♥ ∞ ♥ ∞ ♥ ∞ ♥ ∞ ♥ ∞ ♥ ∞ ♥ ∞ ♥ ∞ ♥ ∞ ♥ ∞ ♥ ∞ ♥ ∞ ♥ ∞ ♥

Dreams may come, dreams may go;
But the dreams within my heart only I truly know;
We can believe in our dreams or let them pass;
But the dreams filled with love & faith are the dreams that last;
Believing in my dreams & a power so much greater than I;
Limits the possibility of my dreams passing me by.

∞ ♥ ∞ ♥ ∞ ♥ ∞ ♥ ∞ ♥ ∞ ♥ ∞ ♥ ∞ ♥ ∞ ♥ ∞ ♥ ∞ ♥ ∞ ♥ ∞ ♥ ∞ ♥ ∞ ♥ ∞ ♥

At the start of my day as it is begun;
I am grateful for the blessing of the morning Sun;
At the end of my day after work and / or fun;
I am grateful for all I received as my day is done.

∞ ♥ ∞ ♥ ∞ ♥ ∞ ♥ ∞ ♥ ∞ ♥ ∞ ♥ ∞ ♥ ∞ ♥ ∞ ♥ ∞ ♥ ∞ ♥ ∞ ♥ ∞ ♥ ∞ ♥ ∞ ♥

The fires within me burn strong & bright;
From the depth of my soul a passion for life it ignites.

Good morning world;
And where today would you like to be hurled;
Go ahead & pick a card;
No one said life had to be hard;
"Deuces are wild" is todays' game of chance;
So what will it be, sunshine & rainbows, maybe a pot of gold, friends
& family, love & romance.

Father, Angels, Masters above;
Spirits & Guardians of this earth, I call to you for your assistance in love;
To deliver this message where it is meant to be;
Carrying the words of love sent from me.

∞ ♥ ∞ ♥ ∞ ♥ ∞ ♥ ∞ ♥ ∞ ♥ ∞ ♥ ∞ ♥ ∞ ♥ ∞ ♥ ∞ ♥ ∞ ♥ ∞ ♥ ∞ ♥ ∞ ♥ ∞ ♥

I believe prayers & wishes do get answered & come true;

Maybe not as you expected but still they are right in front of you;

Some needing your assistance before you may in entirety the blessings reap;

Truly amazing how much easier challenges may be when on the right path you keep.

∞ ♥ ∞ ♥ ∞ ♥ ∞ ♥ ∞ ♥ ∞ ♥ ∞ ♥ ∞ ♥ ∞ ♥ ∞ ♥ ∞ ♥ ∞ ♥ ∞ ♥ ∞ ♥ ∞ ♥

Father, how I love thee, let me count the ways;

Grateful for every blessing you give throughout my love filled days;

Grateful for the strength you give to me in body & mind;

Grateful for your love, for it is truly everywhere I find;

Grateful for my open mind & heart guiding me to the ultimate goal;

Grateful for all wisdom & knowledge held & felt from the depths of my soul;

Grateful eternally for love & light filled blessings in all of my days;

Father, how I love thee, let me count the ways.

∞ ♥ ∞ ♥ ∞ ♥ ∞ ♥ ∞ ♥ ∞ ♥ ∞ ♥ ∞ ♥ ∞ ♥ ∞ ♥ ∞ ♥ ∞ ♥ ∞ ♥ ∞ ♥ ∞ ♥

There is a man in my dreams, that comes to me;

Within my heart knowing everything works out perfectly as it is meant to be;

Love filled days, nights of passion & fire;

This man of my dreams is truly my hearts' desire.

∞ ♥ ∞ ♥ ∞ ♥ ∞ ♥ ∞ ♥ ∞ ♥ ∞ ♥ ∞ ♥ ∞ ♥ ∞ ♥ ∞ ♥ ∞ ♥ ∞ ♥ ∞ ♥ ∞ ♥

Always believe;
Believe & So It Shall Be;
With some Dreams the only thing you can do;
IS Believe & they come true.

Is there something within you creating great desire;
Something within fueling a passionate fire;
Then go out & get it, the path will be made known;
Through your mind, heart & spirit, the way will be shown;
Trusting in Faith & Love that is pure;
Believing with all your heart & soul then desires are fulfilled for sure;
There must always be an effort on your part;
Everything goes right when you follow your heart.

A clear blue sky & sunshine are given to celebrate this last day in June;
Six months of the year have come & gone for me much to fast;
Grateful for each moment, all having been filled with love, under the sun, stars & moon;
Understanding that which I give is returned to me, therefore, my future is my past.

∞ ♥ ∞ ♥ ∞ ♥ ∞ ♥ ∞ ♥ ∞ ♥ ∞ ♥ ∞ ♥ ∞ ♥ ∞ ♥ ∞ ♥ ∞ ♥ ∞ ♥ ∞ ♥ ∞ ♥

If we know our lifes' destination, isn't it best we enjoy our journey on our way there;

Blessings of love fill every moment along the way, isn't it best we enjoy each, as with our loved ones, family, friend or stranger, those blessings we share.

∞ ♥ ∞ ♥ ∞ ♥ ∞ ♥ ∞ ♥ ∞ ♥ ∞ ♥ ∞ ♥ ∞ ♥ ∞ ♥ ∞ ♥ ∞ ♥ ∞ ♥ ∞ ♥ ∞ ♥ ∞ ♥

I am curious, if you were given a second chance in life, what would it be;

Would you choose to be with your love of a lifetime or live wild & free.

∞ ♥ ∞ ♥ ∞ ♥ ∞ ♥ ∞ ♥ ∞ ♥ ∞ ♥ ∞ ♥ ∞ ♥ ∞ ♥ ∞ ♥ ∞ ♥ ∞ ♥ ∞ ♥ ∞ ♥ ∞ ♥

Love is the light that shines within;

Love is the healer, heal thyself is the best place to begin;

Love is the provider of nourishment for my soul;

Love is the strength & courage that takes me where I need to go;

Love is the truth that guides my way;

Love is the faith that takes me to my Father, day after day.

∞ ♥ ∞ ♥ ∞ ♥ ∞ ♥ ∞ ♥ ∞ ♥ ∞ ♥ ∞ ♥ ∞ ♥ ∞ ♥ ∞ ♥ ∞ ♥ ∞ ♥ ∞ ♥ ∞ ♥ ∞ ♥

Day by day I live as I know I should;

To have my dreams be my reality—oh I wish they would;

Life continues on as it is meant to be;

My desires continue to grow, as time will allow, to have you next to me.

Dragonflies & Flutterbies dance in the morning light;

Touching my heart, my spirit, filling me with awe at the sight.

∞♥∞♥∞♥∞♥∞♥∞♥∞♥∞♥∞♥∞♥∞♥∞♥∞♥∞♥∞♥∞♥

I can't help but wonder if you think of me as I think of you;

If given a chance, what choices would we make, what things would we do;

Was it your thoughts of me that had drawn me back to you;

What lies on the path before us, the unknown in itself brings with it, adventure true.

∞♥∞♥∞♥∞♥∞♥∞♥∞♥∞♥∞♥∞♥∞♥∞♥∞♥∞♥∞♥∞♥

Understanding life has complications, challenges of its own;
Steadily I continue on living, walking the path I am shown;
Each day an adventure as it unfolds;
Excitement fills me as I realize possibilities & blessings the future holds.

∞ ♥ ∞ ♥ ∞ ♥ ∞ ♥ ∞ ♥ ∞ ♥ ∞ ♥ ∞ ♥ ∞ ♥ ∞ ♥ ∞ ♥ ∞ ♥ ∞ ♥ ∞ ♥ ∞ ♥ ∞ ♥ ∞ ♥

In truth, being honest & straight forward is all I have ever known;
Saying what needs to be said, staying much the same as I have grown;
Some say it is a good thing, others believe it is not so good, holding it all inside feels so unnatural to me;
So through truths revealed, I set myself free;
Trusting all is & shall be exactly as it is meant to be.

∞ ♥ ∞ ♥ ∞ ♥ ∞ ♥ ∞ ♥ ∞ ♥ ∞ ♥ ∞ ♥ ∞ ♥ ∞ ♥ ∞ ♥ ∞ ♥ ∞ ♥ ∞ ♥ ∞ ♥ ∞ ♥ ∞ ♥

One love, One moment, One hour, One day, One life;
Becoming One with all shall end all strife;
One love given to all of creation;
One for All, All for One, a time of celebration.

∞ ♥ ∞ ♥ ∞ ♥ ∞ ♥ ∞ ♥ ∞ ♥ ∞ ♥ ∞ ♥ ∞ ♥ ∞ ♥ ∞ ♥ ∞ ♥ ∞ ♥ ∞ ♥ ∞ ♥ ∞ ♥ ∞ ♥

Like a candle in the wind, my spirit loves to dance;

Illuminating & swaying in rhythm by choice not by chance;

Finding love in all in life, people, events, creation;

Having Faith through Love & Truth, we make the best of any situation.

∞♥∞♥∞♥∞♥∞♥∞♥∞♥∞♥∞♥∞♥∞♥∞♥∞♥∞♥∞♥∞♥∞♥

A gentle mist envelopes the land on a calm yet breezy night;

A midnight sky overflowing with glimmering stars as they share their light;

Their light like love capable of traveling throughout time & space;

While here, now wrapped in this beauty, I too, travel to another place.

∞♥∞♥∞♥∞♥∞♥∞♥∞♥∞♥∞♥∞♥∞♥∞♥∞♥∞♥∞♥∞♥∞♥

It is a magical, mystical night now at hand;

Stars brightly shining above, while below mist covers the land;

As with light, Love transcends all time & space;

A shiver runs through me as I comprehend such beauty & grace.

∞♥∞♥∞♥∞♥∞♥∞♥∞♥∞♥∞♥∞♥∞♥∞♥∞♥∞♥∞♥∞♥∞♥

Blessed beyond measure from the moment of birth;
Blessings given freely by Angels from heaven & earth;
Listening to the whispers from Angels above;
Turning over all in my life to be surrounded in love;
Taking that which is wrong making it right;
Living in Faith day & night.

∞ ♥ ∞ ♥ ∞ ♥ ∞ ♥ ∞ ♥ ∞ ♥ ∞ ♥ ∞ ♥ ∞ ♥ ∞ ♥ ∞ ♥ ∞ ♥ ∞ ♥ ∞ ♥ ∞ ♥ ∞ ♥ ∞ ♥

Bumps & bruises come & go;
Heartache is a pain we tend not to show;
A morning stroll down the lane;
To help loosen up a body & ease its' pain;

∞ ♥ ∞ ♥ ∞ ♥ ∞ ♥ ∞ ♥ ∞ ♥ ∞ ♥ ∞ ♥ ∞ ♥ ∞ ♥ ∞ ♥ ∞ ♥ ∞ ♥ ∞ ♥ ∞ ♥ ∞ ♥ ∞ ♥

Early in the morning much may be seen;
Deer in the meadow, birds in the air, the dew covered spider webs,
glistening within the grass so green;
Gifts given to us, treasures await for us to see;
Blessings of this earth given to you & to me.

∞ ♥ ∞ ♥ ∞ ♥ ∞ ♥ ∞ ♥ ∞ ♥ ∞ ♥ ∞ ♥ ∞ ♥ ∞ ♥ ∞ ♥ ∞ ♥ ∞ ♥ ∞ ♥ ∞ ♥ ∞ ♥ ∞ ♥

"Always towards the light Lil' One;"
Simple words ring truth as this day is begun
In the shadows & darkness one may lose their way;
In the light one finds truth, protection & love shall always stay.

∞ ♥ ∞ ♥ ∞ ♥ ∞ ♥ ∞ ♥ ∞ ♥ ∞ ♥ ∞ ♥ ∞ ♥ ∞ ♥ ∞ ♥ ∞ ♥ ∞ ♥ ∞ ♥ ∞ ♥ ∞ ♥

A cool morning breeze, a crispness in the air;
In the early hours a scent of summer lingers there;
My trusting companion by my side, venturing out in the dark;
Serenaded by some owls & in the distance a dog's bark;
My soul is set free as I lose myself in the velvety star filled sky;
Amazed by the grandeur & treasure that is before my eyes.

∞ ♥ ∞ ♥ ∞ ♥ ∞ ♥ ∞ ♥ ∞ ♥ ∞ ♥ ∞ ♥ ∞ ♥ ∞ ♥ ∞ ♥ ∞ ♥ ∞ ♥ ∞ ♥ ∞ ♥ ∞ ♥

Blessed be in love & light as grace & beauty fills thy sight;
Blessed be in courage & strength as one fulfills thy destiny at length;
Blessed be in life, one & all;
As creation is interconnected great & small.

∞ ♥ ∞ ♥ ∞ ♥ ∞ ♥ ∞ ♥ ∞ ♥ ∞ ♥ ∞ ♥ ∞ ♥ ∞ ♥ ∞ ♥ ∞ ♥ ∞ ♥ ∞ ♥ ∞ ♥ ∞ ♥

There is a magic in the air, it whispers through the trees;
A soft gentle rain with a cool morning breeze;
Much may be seen on a day like today;
Wishes coming true as they travel your way.

∞ ♥ ∞ ♥ ∞ ♥ ∞ ♥ ∞ ♥ ∞ ♥ ∞ ♥ ∞ ♥ ∞ ♥ ∞ ♥ ∞ ♥ ∞ ♥ ∞ ♥ ∞ ♥ ∞ ♥ ∞ ♥

A restlessness I experienced during the night;
In silent lucidity, dreams were my minds delight;
A deeper sleep I was not to attain;
It seems in control of my dreams my mind wished to remain;
To awaken tired after slumber without rest;
A battle between mind & body as though they put each other to a test.

∞ ♥ ∞ ♥ ∞ ♥ ∞ ♥ ∞ ♥ ∞ ♥ ∞ ♥ ∞ ♥ ∞ ♥ ∞ ♥ ∞ ♥ ∞ ♥ ∞ ♥ ∞ ♥ ∞ ♥ ∞ ♥

My days are long, nights are short or so they seem;
Nights are long enough for a pleasant dream;
A subconscious mind has much to reveal;
Day & Night to live my life in zeal.

∞ ♥ ∞ ♥ ∞ ♥ ∞ ♥ ∞ ♥ ∞ ♥ ∞ ♥ ∞ ♥ ∞ ♥ ∞ ♥ ∞ ♥ ∞ ♥ ∞ ♥ ∞ ♥ ∞ ♥ ∞ ♥

Everything works out as it is meant to be;

When following the right path the steps are easy to see;

Always with some effort we must do our part;

When it is meant to be, it comes together with ease right from the start;

Like pieces of a puzzle fitting snuggly side by side, then life is good;

But when we force things to come together, distorting & creating havoc, it does not allow life to be as it should.

The waters of life are calm & dark;

Look into the depths & find the spark;

Allow the flame to grow strong, fed by the winds of change;

The winds shall guide your course on earth, just as prearranged;

While on earth find the rhythm calling to you;

Life is simple & like water flows naturally when we allow it to.

There is a child within that wishes to play;

So walk in the rain, jump in puddles, or enjoy the bright sunshiny day;

Enjoy life & have some fun;

Who knows a marvelous adventure may have just begun.

When we get what we give day to day;

If we live through deceit, calculations & manipulation, we need to expect that to come our way;

Just as if we live through truth, love & honor, it will be returned each day;

The right thing may be harder to do, but much easier in the long run, choice is always yours along with a price to pay.

∞ ♥ ∞ ♥ ∞ ♥ ∞ ♥ ∞ ♥ ∞ ♥ ∞ ♥ ∞ ♥ ∞ ♥ ∞ ♥ ∞ ♥ ∞ ♥ ∞ ♥ ∞ ♥ ∞ ♥ ∞ ♥

Forever grateful for the love & light that fills my life;

Grateful for the abundance of all the good & for the lack of strife;

Enjoying each moment by sharing love & laughter;

Living life to the fullest, while my dreams I go after;

Harming no other along the way;

Remaining accountable for all I think, do, feel & say.

∞ ♥ ∞ ♥ ∞ ♥ ∞ ♥ ∞ ♥ ∞ ♥ ∞ ♥ ∞ ♥ ∞ ♥ ∞ ♥ ∞ ♥ ∞ ♥ ∞ ♥ ∞ ♥ ∞ ♥ ∞ ♥

So much to do on this gorgeous day;

Work needs to be done, yet I want to play.

∞ ♥ ∞ ♥ ∞ ♥ ∞ ♥ ∞ ♥ ∞ ♥ ∞ ♥ ∞ ♥ ∞ ♥ ∞ ♥ ∞ ♥ ∞ ♥ ∞ ♥ ∞ ♥ ∞ ♥ ∞ ♥

Whether in the light of day or the dark of night;

Always follow your heart & do what is right;

"You get what you give", I heard in a dream—even they remind me of

lifes' lessons learned;

Give your best, make each day count leading you to good fortune earned.

Through love of another given a second chance;

As things work out to share this dance;

Taking nothing for granted yet know it is meant to be;

Finding love in gifts given, right in front of thee.

There is a quiet, a oneness as the day is begun;

Just as dew kisses a rose, each morning is kissed by the sun;

As I remain in awe of the creation I witness each day;

In love, I worship the Creator as it is love that guides my way.

∞ ♥ ∞ ♥ ∞ ♥ ∞ ♥ ∞ ♥ ∞ ♥ ∞ ♥ ∞ ♥ ∞ ♥ ∞ ♥ ∞ ♥ ∞ ♥ ∞ ♥ ∞ ♥ ∞ ♥ ∞ ♥ ∞ ♥

On the day you were born, the heavens did dance;
A blessing indeed as your soul, in life, took this chance;
As the stars aligned in perfect harmony;
So you may become exactly who you are meant to be;
A gem, unique & beautiful, in your own special way;
Blessed be always & especially today.

∞ ♥ ∞ ♥ ∞ ♥ ∞ ♥ ∞ ♥ ∞ ♥ ∞ ♥ ∞ ♥ ∞ ♥ ∞ ♥ ∞ ♥ ∞ ♥ ∞ ♥ ∞ ♥ ∞ ♥ ∞ ♥

Feel & know all in this life that you desire;
Fueled by lifes' passion, your inner fire;
Let love guide your heart along the way;
Remain open to receive all blessings every day.

∞ ♥ ∞ ♥ ∞ ♥ ∞ ♥ ∞ ♥ ∞ ♥ ∞ ♥ ∞ ♥ ∞ ♥ ∞ ♥ ∞ ♥ ∞ ♥ ∞ ♥ ∞ ♥ ∞ ♥ ∞ ♥

Each soul is as unique as a gem with flaws** (if you will) & the ability to sparkle & shine;

Like a diamond in the rough becoming more precious with the passage of time;

Looking beyond the flaws (again if you will) we may see all the beauty that lies within;

Be it ourselves or another this acceptance allows unconditional love to begin.

**[to me "flaw" meaning a unique characteristic something all our own, something making us like no other in positive ways, perhaps seen differently by another—not perfect—imperfectly perfect]

A life lived, choices made over many years;

Choices that have brought much love, laughter & tears;

Expectations of others often left unmet;

Yet a life lived with no regret;

Am I to live out life as another would choose;

To not have a passion for life is what I would lose.

To feel hated by so many, so misunderstood;
I have always loved as best I could;
To be judged for living a life uncontrolled by others;
Choosing not to live behind closed doors & shutters.

∞ ♥ ∞ ♥ ∞ ♥ ∞ ♥ ∞ ♥ ∞ ♥ ∞ ♥ ∞ ♥ ∞ ♥ ∞ ♥ ∞ ♥ ∞ ♥ ∞ ♥ ∞ ♥ ∞ ♥ ∞ ♥

For all others the best in life for them is what I pray;
Exactly what that is to be, only our Father can say;
Freely we give & freely we take;
All choices in our life through freewill we make;
Whether to Bless or curse the choice is yours;
Remember whatever is sent out is returned to your doors.

∞ ♥ ∞ ♥ ∞ ♥ ∞ ♥ ∞ ♥ ∞ ♥ ∞ ♥ ∞ ♥ ∞ ♥ ∞ ♥ ∞ ♥ ∞ ♥ ∞ ♥ ∞ ♥ ∞ ♥ ∞ ♥

There is something I ask for almost every day;
"Allow me to see All & Allow All to see me";
With heartfelt gratitude these words I pray;
To be protected by love & truth to always be.

∞ ♥ ∞ ♥ ∞ ♥ ∞ ♥ ∞ ♥ ∞ ♥ ∞ ♥ ∞ ♥ ∞ ♥ ∞ ♥ ∞ ♥ ∞ ♥ ∞ ♥ ∞ ♥ ∞ ♥ ∞ ♥

Rise, Phoenix, Rise from the ashes, take flight;

With the end comes new beginnings all part of lifes' delight;

A mystical new journey now lies in front of you;

Let your heart be your guide in all you think, say & do;

Rise, Phoenix, Rise, spread your beautiful wings;

Find the magic within, listen as your mind, heart & soul as one now sings.

∞ ♥ ∞ ♥ ∞ ♥ ∞ ♥ ∞ ♥ ∞ ♥ ∞ ♥ ∞ ♥ ∞ ♥ ∞ ♥ ∞ ♥ ∞ ♥ ∞ ♥ ∞ ♥ ∞ ♥ ∞ ♥ ∞ ♥

When you have a dilemma, have to make a choice;

Listen to the guiding of that small inner voice;

For in truth it will lead to the path that is right;

Then watch as everything comes together perfectly, in it delight.

∞ ♥ ∞ ♥ ∞ ♥ ∞ ♥ ∞ ♥ ∞ ♥ ∞ ♥ ∞ ♥ ∞ ♥ ∞ ♥ ∞ ♥ ∞ ♥ ∞ ♥ ∞ ♥ ∞ ♥ ∞ ♥

Holding expectations of others disappointment shall be at hand;

Expectations of myself shall be greater than most may understand.

∞ ♥ ∞ ♥ ∞ ♥ ∞ ♥ ∞ ♥ ∞ ♥ ∞ ♥ ∞ ♥ ∞ ♥ ∞ ♥ ∞ ♥ ∞ ♥ ∞ ♥ ∞ ♥ ∞ ♥ ∞ ♥

There is much in this world we may not understand;

Life changes with every breath, every smile, every time we lend a hand;

Each thought, word or action, let them be honest, heartfelt & true;

Being one in mind, heart & soul, there is much to accomplish, fulfilling

dreams & destiny now that lays before you.

∞ ♥ ∞ ♥ ∞ ♥ ∞ ♥ ∞ ♥ ∞ ♥ ∞ ♥ ∞ ♥ ∞ ♥ ∞ ♥ ∞ ♥ ∞ ♥ ∞ ♥ ∞ ♥ ∞ ♥ ∞ ♥ ∞ ♥

As I gaze at the beauty before me;

One so different from the others I see;

Perfectly, imperfect, wild & free;

Exactly as it was created & meant to be.

∞ ♥ ∞ ♥ ∞ ♥ ∞ ♥ ∞ ♥ ∞ ♥ ∞ ♥ ∞ ♥ ∞ ♥ ∞ ♥ ∞ ♥ ∞ ♥ ∞ ♥ ∞ ♥ ∞ ♥ ∞ ♥ ∞ ♥

Where you lead me, I shall follow;

For without you in my life, I am simply hollow.

∞ ♥ ∞ ♥ ∞ ♥ ∞ ♥ ∞ ♥ ∞ ♥ ∞ ♥ ∞ ♥ ∞ ♥ ∞ ♥ ∞ ♥ ∞ ♥ ∞ ♥ ∞ ♥ ∞ ♥ ∞ ♥ ∞ ♥

Mo Chuisle, Mo Chroi

∞ ♥ ∞ ♥ ∞ ♥ ∞ ♥ ∞ ♥ ∞ ♥ ∞ ♥ ∞ ♥ ∞ ♥ ∞ ♥ ∞ ♥ ∞ ♥ ∞ ♥ ∞ ♥ ∞ ♥ ∞ ♥ ∞ ♥

The pulse of my heart forever to be;
A life with you & your love is my reality;
Through you I find strength & courage to carry on;
I am yours, you have taught me a beautiful new song.

∞ ♥ ∞ ♥ ∞ ♥ ∞ ♥ ∞ ♥ ∞ ♥ ∞ ♥ ∞ ♥ ∞ ♥ ∞ ♥ ∞ ♥ ∞ ♥ ∞ ♥ ∞ ♥ ∞ ♥ ∞ ♥ ∞ ♥

My mind runs rampant with thoughts this day;
As if it cannot decide to work or play;
Choices at hand, decisions to make;
Grateful for the guidance leading to the road I need take.

∞ ♥ ∞ ♥ ∞ ♥ ∞ ♥ ∞ ♥ ∞ ♥ ∞ ♥ ∞ ♥ ∞ ♥ ∞ ♥ ∞ ♥ ∞ ♥ ∞ ♥ ∞ ♥ ∞ ♥ ∞ ♥ ∞ ♥

The harshness of the world can be washed away by a gentle rain;
Calm & soothing, allowing time to slow down in stillness for a while
to remain.

∞ ♥ ∞ ♥ ∞ ♥ ∞ ♥ ∞ ♥ ∞ ♥ ∞ ♥ ∞ ♥ ∞ ♥ ∞ ♥ ∞ ♥ ∞ ♥ ∞ ♥ ∞ ♥ ∞ ♥ ∞ ♥ ∞ ♥

Good friends, good laughter, good medicine for the soul;
Good times, good memories, good life the ultimate goal.

When you look in the mirror what do you see;
Within the reflection is it only you or can you see part of me;
In reality we are all connected, one & the same;
Within each we hold the living flame;
That is why we have the universal rule;
Treat another as you wish to be treated, what you give is returned, so don't be a fool.

(The mind & body, mere containers of the soul for a while; think kindly of yourself & others, act gently with mind & soul, share a smile)

Faith makes anything possible, Hope helps you remain steadfast while your dreams come true;
Love is the guiding light that leads your heart in all you do;
Like the mind, body & soul, the three must be one;
Live in Faith, Hope & Love as each day is begun.

I find the simplest things in life for me hold the most pleasure;

Morning coffee on the deck, a few kind words, or a smile from a friend

or stranger;

Moments of time, given & received as a gift, nature in its' grandeur are

what I most treasure.

∞ ♥ ∞ ♥ ∞ ♥ ∞ ♥ ∞ ♥ ∞ ♥ ∞ ♥ ∞ ♥ ∞ ♥ ∞ ♥ ∞ ♥ ∞ ♥ ∞ ♥ ∞ ♥ ∞ ♥ ∞ ♥ ∞ ♥

Blessings abound as this new day is begun;

New beginnings arrive with the rising sun;

As the morning star shines its light;

This day & the future are beautiful & bright.

∞ ♥ ∞ ♥ ∞ ♥ ∞ ♥ ∞ ♥ ∞ ♥ ∞ ♥ ∞ ♥ ∞ ♥ ∞ ♥ ∞ ♥ ∞ ♥ ∞ ♥ ∞ ♥ ∞ ♥ ∞ ♥ ∞ ♥

Open your mind, open your heart;

With Love & Laughter is a great way to start;

Know your life is good & so it shall be;

Always grateful for the love & blessings you feel & see.

∞ ♥ ∞ ♥ ∞ ♥ ∞ ♥ ∞ ♥ ∞ ♥ ∞ ♥ ∞ ♥ ∞ ♥ ∞ ♥ ∞ ♥ ∞ ♥ ∞ ♥ ∞ ♥ ∞ ♥ ∞ ♥ ∞ ♥

The nectars of life may be bitter or sweet;

Life gives many lessons to learn & grow in each new day we greet;

Live & give without regret, harming no one, without blame, shame or guilt, to enjoy Lifes' experiences as an undeniable treat.

∞ ♥ ∞ ♥ ∞ ♥ ∞ ♥ ∞ ♥ ∞ ♥ ∞ ♥ ∞ ♥ ∞ ♥ ∞ ♥ ∞ ♥ ∞ ♥ ∞ ♥ ∞ ♥ ∞ ♥ ∞ ♥

I believe . . .

Everything happens for a reason;

I may not immediately understand, although I know it is perfect timing in the perfect season ☺

Got Faith?

∞ ♥ ∞ ♥ ∞ ♥ ∞ ♥ ∞ ♥ ∞ ♥ ∞ ♥ ∞ ♥ ∞ ♥ ∞ ♥ ∞ ♥ ∞ ♥ ∞ ♥ ∞ ♥ ∞ ♥ ∞ ♥

Started with one, but soon shall have three;

A commitment to love, many blessings for me;

Added protection with loyalty, gifts of love;

Seeing blessings in threes sent from heaven above;

Being receptive of what was requested when it is delivered to your door;

Acceptance with heart & soul, leaves you open to receive even more.

∞ ♥ ∞ ♥ ∞ ♥ ∞ ♥ ∞ ♥ ∞ ♥ ∞ ♥ ∞ ♥ ∞ ♥ ∞ ♥ ∞ ♥ ∞ ♥ ∞ ♥ ∞ ♥ ∞ ♥ ∞ ♥

Prayers, requests for others & myself sent out into the night;

Asked for signs & they have begun to be given with mornings light;

Ask & it shall be given, seek & ye shall find;

Believe & so it shall be, needing only an open heart & open mind.

∞ ♥ ∞ ♥ ∞ ♥ ∞ ♥ ∞ ♥ ∞ ♥ ∞ ♥ ∞ ♥ ∞ ♥ ∞ ♥ ∞ ♥ ∞ ♥ ∞ ♥ ∞ ♥ ∞ ♥ ∞ ♥

Divine order creating Chaos in life, in each day;

Or perhaps it is Chaos that creates Divine order through freewill in some way.

∞ ♥ ∞ ♥ ∞ ♥ ∞ ♥ ∞ ♥ ∞ ♥ ∞ ♥ ∞ ♥ ∞ ♥ ∞ ♥ ∞ ♥ ∞ ♥ ∞ ♥ ∞ ♥ ∞ ♥ ∞ ♥

Blessings come in many guises, great & small;

Messages given through the gift of a dog or maybe a call;

Life is good if we allow it to be;

There is more to this life than we generally see.

∞ ♥ ∞ ♥ ∞ ♥ ∞ ♥ ∞ ♥ ∞ ♥ ∞ ♥ ∞ ♥ ∞ ♥ ∞ ♥ ∞ ♥ ∞ ♥ ∞ ♥ ∞ ♥ ∞ ♥ ∞ ♥

Outside with my companions a new day begun;

Seeking new adventures under the clouds & the sun;

As always life can bring challenges as well as a lot of fun.

∞ ♥ ∞ ♥ ∞ ♥ ∞ ♥ ∞ ♥ ∞ ♥ ∞ ♥ ∞ ♥ ∞ ♥ ∞ ♥ ∞ ♥ ∞ ♥ ∞ ♥ ∞ ♥ ∞ ♥ ∞ ♥

A friend once said, when God talks to you, He says things twice;
I have learned to listen closely or I may pay a price;
For throughout my years I have come to understand;
My needs are always met, my dreams do come true, while I continue
my quest, walking in His light across this beautiful land.

∞ ♥ ∞ ♥ ∞ ♥ ∞ ♥ ∞ ♥ ∞ ♥ ∞ ♥ ∞ ♥ ∞ ♥ ∞ ♥ ∞ ♥ ∞ ♥ ∞ ♥ ∞ ♥ ∞ ♥ ∞ ♥ ∞ ♥

Sister moon high above me;
Whisper in my dreams, tell me what it is you see;
A perfect view of this world & so much more;
A beacon placed at heavens' door;
Moon so beautiful as I gaze upon thee;
Whisper softly, tell me what you see.

∞ ♥ ∞ ♥ ∞ ♥ ∞ ♥ ∞ ♥ ∞ ♥ ∞ ♥ ∞ ♥ ∞ ♥ ∞ ♥ ∞ ♥ ∞ ♥ ∞ ♥ ∞ ♥ ∞ ♥ ∞ ♥ ∞ ♥

There is something calling to me from the depths of my soul;
Something so strong, I feel it makes me whole;
An adventure in life, just outside my door;
Living life to its' fullest in truth, love & light leaves me asking for more.

∞ ♥ ∞ ♥ ∞ ♥ ∞ ♥ ∞ ♥ ∞ ♥ ∞ ♥ ∞ ♥ ∞ ♥ ∞ ♥ ∞ ♥ ∞ ♥ ∞ ♥ ∞ ♥ ∞ ♥ ∞ ♥ ∞ ♥

Mo Chuisle

Mo Chroi

The pulse of my heart, forever to be.

Grateful for the brand new day I find;

I pray for patience & a heart that is kind;

Love & light to guide my way;

Wisdom, courage & strength to fill my day.

With the spirit of a Dragon, I now take wing;

For it is my spirit that allows my soul to sing;

Like the Eagle in the heavens, to new heights I shall soar;

Like the Panther on the earth I shall travel from shore to shore;

Through this quest in life I shall journey through light & dark;

Undoubtedly at times I shall leave my mark;

The fires within are a passion to live;

Never far from my thoughts, "You get what you give."

∞ ♥ ∞ ♥ ∞ ♥ ∞ ♥ ∞ ♥ ∞ ♥ ∞ ♥ ∞ ♥ ∞ ♥ ∞ ♥ ∞ ♥ ∞ ♥ ∞ ♥ ∞ ♥ ∞ ♥ ∞ ♥

Have you ever noticed when you are in sync with life, everything works
out just right;

No pushing, pulling or shoving to make things fit, no need to put up a fight;

Everything being in perfect union, in the perfect season, whether day
or night.

∞ ♥ ∞ ♥ ∞ ♥ ∞ ♥ ∞ ♥ ∞ ♥ ∞ ♥ ∞ ♥ ∞ ♥ ∞ ♥ ∞ ♥ ∞ ♥ ∞ ♥ ∞ ♥ ∞ ♥

Feels like Autumn's winds now kiss the trees;

While out this morning, there is a cool gentle breeze;

A chill in the air that came in the night;

In love with nature as it gives my heart delight;

Soon Summer's madness shall be done;

Then time for Winter's Narnia & another type of fun.

∞ ♥ ∞ ♥ ∞ ♥ ∞ ♥ ∞ ♥ ∞ ♥ ∞ ♥ ∞ ♥ ∞ ♥ ∞ ♥ ∞ ♥ ∞ ♥ ∞ ♥ ∞ ♥ ∞ ♥

A bid was made to take the blinders off;

But instead you are willing to lay blame, ridicule & scoff;

Had told you once & now tell you again;

"Remember, you are always surrounded by love", sincerely words of a
friend;

Whether you accept it as given is a choice through your own freewill;

Open your mind, open your heart, open your eyes & see, we each pay
a price for we have created our own karmic bill!

∞ ♥ ∞ ♥ ∞ ♥ ∞ ♥ ∞ ♥ ∞ ♥ ∞ ♥ ∞ ♥ ∞ ♥ ∞ ♥ ∞ ♥ ∞ ♥ ∞ ♥ ∞ ♥ ∞ ♥

I love my life in every way;

Simplest of joys in each day;

Moment to moment I continue to smile;

Just drinking it in all the while;

Like now, the sun is shining bright, bringing warmth to the air;

As Humming birds joyously do their aerial dance without a care.

A call to battle, to do what is right;

To stand your ground, to fight a good fight;

Honesty not deceit, truth not lies;

Love not hate, reach for the skies;

Blessings abound while on a path that is true;

As always with having freewill, the choice is up to you.

Find the rhythm of life everywhere you go;
Travel the depths within, there is much for you to know;
Love & accept yourself as you continue to learn & grow;
Unveil the light within, release it, let it glow.

∞ ♥ ∞ ♥ ∞ ♥ ∞ ♥ ∞ ♥ ∞ ♥ ∞ ♥ ∞ ♥ ∞ ♥ ∞ ♥ ∞ ♥ ∞ ♥ ∞ ♥ ∞ ♥ ∞ ♥ ∞ ♥

Sisters not by blood, sisters by choice;
Uncanny how they seem to have a similar voice;
Acceptance for each other out of love not fear;
With the passage of time, a love held dear.

∞ ♥ ∞ ♥ ∞ ♥ ∞ ♥ ∞ ♥ ∞ ♥ ∞ ♥ ∞ ♥ ∞ ♥ ∞ ♥ ∞ ♥ ∞ ♥ ∞ ♥ ∞ ♥ ∞ ♥ ∞ ♥

Humming birds, Dragonflies with a Flicker & Eagle to join the brew;
Joy, light & rhythm are instant karma coming back to you.

∞ ♥ ∞ ♥ ∞ ♥ ∞ ♥ ∞ ♥ ∞ ♥ ∞ ♥ ∞ ♥ ∞ ♥ ∞ ♥ ∞ ♥ ∞ ♥ ∞ ♥ ∞ ♥ ∞ ♥ ∞ ♥

The future is the past & soon we shall see;

Blessings through love, gifts given to you & me;

A future bright, full of good cheer;

A past of lessons learned full of memories we hold dear.

Cherish the gift of the present, for tomorrow we know not what it brings;

Creating love in all we are, lessens the possible stings;

Love, laughter, joys in life & forgiveness to those who may cause some pain;

Sorrows & pain shall be forgotten but the memories of love & laughter forever remain.

Simple joys, simple pleasures;

Absolutely, I admit, are my life's greatest treasures;

A hug from a friend, a conversation with someone I love;

Blessings of this earth sent from heaven above;

So Grateful for each moment in this blessed life I live;

Grateful for each adventure, accepting the truth, we get out of life that which we give.

∞♥∞♥∞♥∞♥∞♥∞♥∞♥∞♥∞♥∞♥∞♥∞♥∞♥∞♥∞♥

It is not easy to live life fulfilling the expectation of another;

Whether they are lover, friend, family . . . Sister or brother;

Love unconditionally, harm no other, with no guilt, no shame, no blame, no judgment, no regrets, I live with these rules I have placed on myself;

The opinions of others, I place on a shelf;

I alone walk in my shoes;

Therefore, I alone must pay the price, while walking the path that I willingly choose.

∞ ♥ ∞ ♥ ∞ ♥ ∞ ♥ ∞ ♥ ∞ ♥ ∞ ♥ ∞ ♥ ∞ ♥ ∞ ♥ ∞ ♥ ∞ ♥ ∞ ♥ ∞ ♥ ∞ ♥ ∞ ♥ ∞ ♥

Everything is changing some times fast, some times slow;

Everything has a season, its' own special time;

In unison with life, knowing exactly when & where to go;

Beauty abounds, like sunshine & rainbows, treasures sublime.

∞ ♥ ∞ ♥ ∞ ♥ ∞ ♥ ∞ ♥ ∞ ♥ ∞ ♥ ∞ ♥ ∞ ♥ ∞ ♥ ∞ ♥ ∞ ♥ ∞ ♥ ∞ ♥ ∞ ♥ ∞ ♥ ∞ ♥

Fall is around the corner, signs are everywhere;

Trees losing their leaves, a chill is in the air;

Harvesting soon to start, to reap what was sown;

Nature gently reminding us of the rules of life we inherently have known.

∞ ♥ ∞ ♥ ∞ ♥ ∞ ♥ ∞ ♥ ∞ ♥ ∞ ♥ ∞ ♥ ∞ ♥ ∞ ♥ ∞ ♥ ∞ ♥ ∞ ♥ ∞ ♥ ∞ ♥ ∞ ♥ ∞ ♥

The simplest things give me smiles;

Such as, thoughts of you across the miles;

Cat playing with the grass, dog laying at my feet;

The feeling of love & peace, my serenity with each new day I greet;

Sunshine & rainbows after a cool mornings' rain;

Understanding always I have nothing to lose & everything to gain.

∞ ♥ ∞ ♥ ∞ ♥ ∞ ♥ ∞ ♥ ∞ ♥ ∞ ♥ ∞ ♥ ∞ ♥ ∞ ♥ ∞ ♥ ∞ ♥ ∞ ♥ ∞ ♥ ∞ ♥ ∞ ♥

So tiny, one of so little mass;

Not even the storms' winds move you from your task;

As you play & feast & move about without a care;

Such joy to watch you dance in the air;

Thank you for reminding me all our needs are met;

And even when facing lifes' storms there is no need to fret.

∞ ♥ ∞ ♥ ∞ ♥ ∞ ♥ ∞ ♥ ∞ ♥ ∞ ♥ ∞ ♥ ∞ ♥ ∞ ♥ ∞ ♥ ∞ ♥ ∞ ♥ ∞ ♥ ∞ ♥ ∞ ♥

Wisdom from the past has come my way, knowledge shared through another sage;

His words as written, I comprehend, as I am one with them page after page.

∞ ♥ ∞ ♥ ∞ ♥ ∞ ♥ ∞ ♥ ∞ ♥ ∞ ♥ ∞ ♥ ∞ ♥ ∞ ♥ ∞ ♥ ∞ ♥ ∞ ♥ ∞ ♥ ∞ ♥ ∞ ♥

She sits alone in silence like a ghost;
As if a sentinel at her post;
Another shall come with the passing of time;
She trusts in life & all that is divine.

∞ ♥ ∞ ♥ ∞ ♥ ∞ ♥ ∞ ♥ ∞ ♥ ∞ ♥ ∞ ♥ ∞ ♥ ∞ ♥ ∞ ♥ ∞ ♥ ∞ ♥ ∞ ♥ ∞ ♥ ∞ ♥ ∞ ♥

Cold & stormy on this summer's day;
As autumn's return now comes this way;
All that is lush & green soon we shall see no more;
As winter comes knocking on autumn's door;
A new season to prepare for the slumber of this earth;
After winters' chills we shall again with spring see earths' rebirth.

∞ ♥ ∞ ♥ ∞ ♥ ∞ ♥ ∞ ♥ ∞ ♥ ∞ ♥ ∞ ♥ ∞ ♥ ∞ ♥ ∞ ♥ ∞ ♥ ∞ ♥ ∞ ♥ ∞ ♥ ∞ ♥ ∞ ♥

A day bright with sunshine, also a moon that is new;
Many thoughts & prayers, I send to you;
May your days be filled with love & your nights give you rest;
With Faith, Wisdom, Strength & Courage pass each of lifes' tests.

∞ ♥ ∞ ♥ ∞ ♥ ∞ ♥ ∞ ♥ ∞ ♥ ∞ ♥ ∞ ♥ ∞ ♥ ∞ ♥ ∞ ♥ ∞ ♥ ∞ ♥ ∞ ♥ ∞ ♥ ∞ ♥ ∞ ♥

The beauty of sunrise I have seen with my eyes;

This morn as reds, pinks, oranges & yellows kissed & blessed the skies;

Many blessings are given to you & me;

With an open heart & open mind gifs of every moment become easy to see.

∞ ♥ ∞ ♥ ∞ ♥ ∞ ♥ ∞ ♥ ∞ ♥ ∞ ♥ ∞ ♥ ∞ ♥ ∞ ♥ ∞ ♥ ∞ ♥ ∞ ♥ ∞ ♥ ∞ ♥ ∞ ♥ ∞ ♥

May you feel His comfort & love as He holds you in His arms;

A promise to love & protect you always, keeping you from all harms;

Trusting He shall take that which is wrong making it right;

For within His heart you are surrounded with purest love & light.

∞ ♥ ∞ ♥ ∞ ♥ ∞ ♥ ∞ ♥ ∞ ♥ ∞ ♥ ∞ ♥ ∞ ♥ ∞ ♥ ∞ ♥ ∞ ♥ ∞ ♥ ∞ ♥ ∞ ♥ ∞ ♥ ∞ ♥

"Spirit Walker" is being whispered gently in my ear;

When I asked why, "you walk among many spirits, man & creature/ animal." Are the next words I hear.

∞ ♥ ∞ ♥ ∞ ♥ ∞ ♥ ∞ ♥ ∞ ♥ ∞ ♥ ∞ ♥ ∞ ♥ ∞ ♥ ∞ ♥ ∞ ♥ ∞ ♥ ∞ ♥ ∞ ♥ ∞ ♥ ∞ ♥

My mind, it wanders to the depths of my soul, to a peace within;
Finding treasures of love for this new day & its' adventures, I now begin;
Work to be done & of course time left to play;
Truly it is the love & laughter that brightens every day.

∞ ♥ ∞ ♥ ∞ ♥ ∞ ♥ ∞ ♥ ∞ ♥ ∞ ♥ ∞ ♥ ∞ ♥ ∞ ♥ ∞ ♥ ∞ ♥ ∞ ♥ ∞ ♥ ∞ ♥ ∞ ♥

A surprise visit from an old friend;
Gifts given through the kindness of words—blessings in life from beginning to end.

∞ ♥ ∞ ♥ ∞ ♥ ∞ ♥ ∞ ♥ ∞ ♥ ∞ ♥ ∞ ♥ ∞ ♥ ∞ ♥ ∞ ♥ ∞ ♥ ∞ ♥ ∞ ♥ ∞ ♥ ∞ ♥

Mid September morn & some branches are already bare;
Gentle rain falls, leaving its' scent in the air;
Transformation has begun, soon there shall be a different view;
Take a moment, look around, drink it in—what is nature telling you.

∞ ♥ ∞ ♥ ∞ ♥ ∞ ♥ ∞ ♥ ∞ ♥ ∞ ♥ ∞ ♥ ∞ ♥ ∞ ♥ ∞ ♥ ∞ ♥ ∞ ♥ ∞ ♥ ∞ ♥ ∞ ♥

The waters run wide, the waters run deep;

The waters of old, many secrets they keep;

The waters are calm, seemingly still;

The waters of life flow freely where they will.

∞ ♥ ∞ ♥ ∞ ♥ ∞ ♥ ∞ ♥ ∞ ♥ ∞ ♥ ∞ ♥ ∞ ♥ ∞ ♥ ∞ ♥ ∞ ♥ ∞ ♥ ∞ ♥ ∞ ♥ ∞ ♥

Say what you mean & mean what you say;

Life is too short to be treated as a game to play;

Enjoy each moment for they quickly pass;

Make each one count & make it last.

∞ ♥ ∞ ♥ ∞ ♥ ∞ ♥ ∞ ♥ ∞ ♥ ∞ ♥ ∞ ♥ ∞ ♥ ∞ ♥ ∞ ♥ ∞ ♥ ∞ ♥ ∞ ♥ ∞ ♥ ∞ ♥

May you always be surrounded by those you hold dear;

May you have a life of happiness, laughter & love that continues on
year after year.

∞ ♥ ∞ ♥ ∞ ♥ ∞ ♥ ∞ ♥ ∞ ♥ ∞ ♥ ∞ ♥ ∞ ♥ ∞ ♥ ∞ ♥ ∞ ♥ ∞ ♥ ∞ ♥ ∞ ♥ ∞ ♥

On this day as you celebrate the day of your birth;

May you find sunshine & rainbows, gifts of the earth;

Always surrounded by those that in your heart you hold dear;

Life filled with much love, laugher & good cheer.

∞ ♥ ∞ ♥ ∞ ♥ ∞ ♥ ∞ ♥ ∞ ♥ ∞ ♥ ∞ ♥ ∞ ♥ ∞ ♥ ∞ ♥ ∞ ♥ ∞ ♥ ∞ ♥ ∞ ♥ ∞ ♥ ∞ ♥

A day of beauty, a day of grace;

Peace & serenity fills this time & space;

Love abounds through laughter & good cheer;

For the dreams within my heart, fulfillment is near.

∞ ♥ ∞ ♥ ∞ ♥ ∞ ♥ ∞ ♥ ∞ ♥ ∞ ♥ ∞ ♥ ∞ ♥ ∞ ♥ ∞ ♥ ∞ ♥ ∞ ♥ ∞ ♥ ∞ ♥ ∞ ♥ ∞ ♥

I desire someone to love, someone to romance;

Someone who best honors the needs of my soul, someone to have a

second chance.

∞ ♥ ∞ ♥ ∞ ♥ ∞ ♥ ∞ ♥ ∞ ♥ ∞ ♥ ∞ ♥ ∞ ♥ ∞ ♥ ∞ ♥ ∞ ♥ ∞ ♥ ∞ ♥ ∞ ♥ ∞ ♥ ∞ ♥

There are these feelings that run to the depths of my soul;

I often wonder, if in truth revealed; of them, will you, ever know;

Seemingly so far away yet remaining forever near;

Within my heart these thoughts, feelings I will ever hold dear.

There is a sadness, a loneliness that I cannot explain;

I have yet to find a way to ease this deep pain;

My thoughts travel to you without understanding why;

From deep within me the tears arise leaving me no other choice but to cry.

∞ ♥ ∞ ♥ ∞ ♥ ∞ ♥ ∞ ♥ ∞ ♥ ∞ ♥ ∞ ♥ ∞ ♥ ∞ ♥ ∞ ♥ ∞ ♥ ∞ ♥ ∞ ♥ ∞ ♥ ∞ ♥ ∞ ♥

I long to be held in my lovers' arms;

Who, is my friend & lover & equal surrounding me always, fulfilling me with his charms;

The one who accepts me for everything I am in every way;

He who honors every need of my soul every moment every day.

∞ ♥ ∞ ♥ ∞ ♥ ∞ ♥ ∞ ♥ ∞ ♥ ∞ ♥ ∞ ♥ ∞ ♥ ∞ ♥ ∞ ♥ ∞ ♥ ∞ ♥ ∞ ♥ ∞ ♥ ∞ ♥ ∞ ♥

With this life people will come, people will go;
Always having touched your soul more than you know;
Some will be with you a lifetime, others only a moment or two;
The traces you leave with them is all up to you.

∞ ♥ ∞ ♥ ∞ ♥ ∞ ♥ ∞ ♥ ∞ ♥ ∞ ♥ ∞ ♥ ∞ ♥ ∞ ♥ ∞ ♥ ∞ ♥ ∞ ♥ ∞ ♥ ∞ ♥ ∞ ♥ ∞ ♥

A foggy, misty, mysterious morning such pleasure for my mind;
A new days journey begun, filled with excitement as I seek new treasures
that await for me to find.

∞ ♥ ∞ ♥ ∞ ♥ ∞ ♥ ∞ ♥ ∞ ♥ ∞ ♥ ∞ ♥ ∞ ♥ ∞ ♥ ∞ ♥ ∞ ♥ ∞ ♥ ∞ ♥ ∞ ♥ ∞ ♥ ∞ ♥

Happy Birthday dear one!!
May you be blessed by every thing good under the stars, moon & sun;
Having a life filled with love, peace, joy & happiness with each days
adventure as it is begun.

∞ ♥ ∞ ♥ ∞ ♥ ∞ ♥ ∞ ♥ ∞ ♥ ∞ ♥ ∞ ♥ ∞ ♥ ∞ ♥ ∞ ♥ ∞ ♥ ∞ ♥ ∞ ♥ ∞ ♥ ∞ ♥ ∞ ♥

To find a day of beauty, after a night of rest;

Everything is transforming, changing for the best;

As a heart beats slowly within a chest;

Journeys continue, the goal is to finish each quest;

With Faith, Love, Strength & Courage to pass each test.

∞ ♥ ∞ ♥ ∞ ♥ ∞ ♥ ∞ ♥ ∞ ♥ ∞ ♥ ∞ ♥ ∞ ♥ ∞ ♥ ∞ ♥ ∞ ♥ ∞ ♥ ∞ ♥ ∞ ♥ ∞ ♥ ∞ ♥

Humming birds & butterflies

A day soon comes when I shall say good-bye;

Knowing you must go I shall not cry;

So many joys & pleasure you have given to me;

As it is with all things in life, you are meant to be free;

As you journey on, your memory I shall hold dear;

Believing you shall come back again to see me here.

Today dear friend is your special day;

May all that is good in life come your way;

May you be surrounded by those that love you, be they family or friend;

May this day hold much love, laughter & joy from beginning to end;

∞ ♥ ∞ ♥ ∞ ♥ ∞ ♥ ∞ ♥ ∞ ♥ ∞ ♥ ∞ ♥ ∞ ♥ ∞ ♥ ∞ ♥ ∞ ♥ ∞ ♥ ∞ ♥ ∞ ♥ ∞ ♥ ∞ ♥

The rains continue to fall, the waters continue to rise;

For my castle to have a moat by the end of this day shall be no surprise;

The rivers' waters run deep, her current is strong;

She is stirring & churning as she quickly moves along.

∞ ♥ ∞ ♥ ∞ ♥ ∞ ♥ ∞ ♥ ∞ ♥ ∞ ♥ ∞ ♥ ∞ ♥ ∞ ♥ ∞ ♥ ∞ ♥ ∞ ♥ ∞ ♥ ∞ ♥ ∞ ♥ ∞ ♥

So much has changed in a matter of hours;

Except my Faith remains, understanding our Creators powers;

As I gaze at the river, widened, running rapid, creating a new dance;

Believing all will be well I stay, for me it is not a matter of chance.

∞ ♥ ∞ ♥ ∞ ♥ ∞ ♥ ∞ ♥ ∞ ♥ ∞ ♥ ∞ ♥ ∞ ♥ ∞ ♥ ∞ ♥ ∞ ♥ ∞ ♥ ∞ ♥ ∞ ♥ ∞ ♥ ∞ ♥

Seeking refuge from the rivers' rage, a blessing I say for thee;

Little one, all shall be just fine, blessed be, blessed be, blessed be;

You shall be safe here, take refuge in this little sanctuary.

From circumstances in life I shall not run;

It is my nature to face them head on;

After the rains I shall see the sun;

Just like after the darkness of night greeted by a glorious dawn.

When I look into your beautiful eyes;

I see a new world, a world of such beauty for which there is no disguise.

Air, Earth, Water & Fire;

With all my heart my true love I desire;

My spirit it calls to him alone;

I request the Sun, Moon & Stars to bring him home;

Let him hear these words I say;

For he alone has my love each & every day;

Air, Earth, Water & Fire;

Bring him quickly to my side, fulfilling our life together is my greatest desire.

A setting sun to the west, simultaneously to the east the moon does rise;

Light transforms to darkness, yielding to the clear starlit skies;

Grateful for the beauty of this earth, I behold with my eyes.

∞ ♥ ∞ ♥ ∞ ♥ ∞ ♥ ∞ ♥ ∞ ♥ ∞ ♥ ∞ ♥ ∞ ♥ ∞ ♥ ∞ ♥ ∞ ♥ ∞ ♥ ∞ ♥ ∞ ♥ ∞ ♥ ∞ ♥

Thinking of my wishes, my dreams can bring tears to my eyes;

God gives me a hug as I watch an Eagle fly to the northern skies;

Believe in dreams & they shall come true;

The desires of my heart bring you to me & me to you.

∞ ♥ ∞ ♥ ∞ ♥ ∞ ♥ ∞ ♥ ∞ ♥ ∞ ♥ ∞ ♥ ∞ ♥ ∞ ♥ ∞ ♥ ∞ ♥ ∞ ♥ ∞ ♥ ∞ ♥ ∞ ♥ ∞ ♥

My loves flies on the wings of an Eagle;

With every beat of my heart, my soul aches for you;

So much that I wish to say, but each whisper do you really hear;

Longing to have you by my side;

Believing in fate & destination in time you shall be with me.

A brand new day, outside a sense of calm & I have a sense of peace within;

As the sun rises to the east the moon is in the west—a thick fog blankets the earth as this day I begin;

An adventure awaits, many joys are to be found;

Blessings of the earth & the heavens, gifts for the heart, the soul, blessings of love are all around.

Gently, she moves, with such grace;

A calmness, yet with a purpose, she continues on from place to place;

She alone knows why, as she journeys along;

Listen closely, hear her sing her sweet song.

∞ ♥ ∞ ♥ ∞ ♥ ∞ ♥ ∞ ♥ ∞ ♥ ∞ ♥ ∞ ♥ ∞ ♥ ∞ ♥ ∞ ♥ ∞ ♥ ∞ ♥ ∞ ♥ ∞ ♥ ∞ ♥ ∞ ♥

To fully experience the joys of today;

One must have known yesterday's sorrows;

Many blessings come day to day;

May yours hold many joys for all of your tomorrows.

∞ ♥ ∞ ♥ ∞ ♥ ∞ ♥ ∞ ♥ ∞ ♥ ∞ ♥ ∞ ♥ ∞ ♥ ∞ ♥ ∞ ♥ ∞ ♥ ∞ ♥ ∞ ♥ ∞ ♥ ∞ ♥ ∞ ♥

Great Sages of this world had/have much wisdom to give;

They taught/teach not only with their words but also by the way they did live;

The gift of freewill to All of creation our Father gave;

Knowing we are accountable, responsible in thought, word & deed, how we behave.

∞ ♥ ∞ ♥ ∞ ♥ ∞ ♥ ∞ ♥ ∞ ♥ ∞ ♥ ∞ ♥ ∞ ♥ ∞ ♥ ∞ ♥ ∞ ♥ ∞ ♥ ∞ ♥ ∞ ♥ ∞ ♥ ∞ ♥

September's end has come too soon;

Its' time to reap what was sown in April, May & June;

Harvests plentiful the rewards shall be;

It is the magic of life, giving blessings to you & me.

∞ ♥ ∞ ♥ ∞ ♥ ∞ ♥ ∞ ♥ ∞ ♥ ∞ ♥ ∞ ♥ ∞ ♥ ∞ ♥ ∞ ♥ ∞ ♥ ∞ ♥ ∞ ♥ ∞ ♥ ∞ ♥ ∞ ♥

First October morn, there is a crisp cool breeze;

As I sit having coffee, seeing my breath, watching leaves fall from the trees;

A prayer I say for many near & far;

My love transcends all of space & time, it matters not where you are.

Earth, it hears winters' call;

Preparing to slumber during this season of fall;

A chill in the air, many leaves on the ground;

Blessings to behold, await to be found;

These changes bring such beauty with a multitude of colors to see;

As with all things in creation, in perfect unison, as it is meant to be.

Peace & serenity greet me this day;

A sky of pink & blue holds a crescent moon;

Frost covered grass & a fog upon the water drifts away;

All to be filled with life very soon.

A gentle fog lifts softly as if beckoned to the skies;
Dancing on sunbeams through the trees with the sunrise;
Waters drift slowly by glistening as it is kissed by the sun;
A calm tranquil day perfectly begun.

∞ ♥ ∞ ♥ ∞ ♥ ∞ ♥ ∞ ♥ ∞ ♥ ∞ ♥ ∞ ♥ ∞ ♥ ∞ ♥ ∞ ♥ ∞ ♥ ∞ ♥ ∞ ♥ ∞ ♥ ∞ ♥

A playful little imp comes bounding in;
Feeling as though she says, "Let the fun begin";
"Come on let's run, come on let's play";
Just as fast as she came in, she now runs away.

∞ ♥ ∞ ♥ ∞ ♥ ∞ ♥ ∞ ♥ ∞ ♥ ∞ ♥ ∞ ♥ ∞ ♥ ∞ ♥ ∞ ♥ ∞ ♥ ∞ ♥ ∞ ♥ ∞ ♥ ∞ ♥

Rainbows dance on the ceiling & walls, like multi colored flames;
Sunlight dances on the water, magic of this life, my soul it tames;
The Gypsy within, she calls to me;
With song & dance, I shall set her free.

∞ ♥ ∞ ♥ ∞ ♥ ∞ ♥ ∞ ♥ ∞ ♥ ∞ ♥ ∞ ♥ ∞ ♥ ∞ ♥ ∞ ♥ ∞ ♥ ∞ ♥ ∞ ♥ ∞ ♥ ∞ ♥

From heaven to earth, a journey of choice made;

To walk the path before me that my soul has laid;

Seeing & understanding the light & love of God in all creation that surrounds me;

Everything is interconnected as He holds all within His heart, with love it is easy to see.

Yesterday, a vision of a Panther I did see;

Eyes wide open, black, beautiful & sleek, I watched as she gently approached me;

Calm, her demeanor, yet her presence like royalty;

To me, she represents love & protection of my children, as well as loyalty;

Fearlessly she will defend & attack in the time of need;

Any with bad intent, shall meet with fang & claw, lest her warning they heed.

Life meanders on at its own chosen pace;

Most times filled with tranquility & others with stillness or haste;

To touch so many inevitably leaving a trace;

Yet life moves on waiting for no one, therefore, one moment I shall not waste.

Like a crystal or a gem many facets have I;

Each uniquely designed by the Potters' hands & a craftsman's eye;

As a prism emits rainbows in light the treasures within cannot hide;

To shine brightly, like stars in the heavens, as a beacon on earth, one & all are meant to abide.

∞ ♥ ∞ ♥ ∞ ♥ ∞ ♥ ∞ ♥ ∞ ♥ ∞ ♥ ∞ ♥ ∞ ♥ ∞ ♥ ∞ ♥ ∞ ♥ ∞ ♥ ∞ ♥ ∞ ♥ ∞ ♥ ∞ ♥

Knock & it shall be open

There are many things in life that are not as they appear to be;

Learning to look under the surface of all things, events, people & places with a greater understanding then in truth we begin to see;

Everything in life changes, some doors will close while others will now open, as we continue searching, desiring more;

Ask & it shall be given, Seek & ye shall find, Live today to its' fullest, for tomorrow we stand at the threshold of a new door.

∞ ♥ ∞ ♥ ∞ ♥ ∞ ♥ ∞ ♥ ∞ ♥ ∞ ♥ ∞ ♥ ∞ ♥ ∞ ♥ ∞ ♥ ∞ ♥ ∞ ♥ ∞ ♥ ∞ ♥ ∞ ♥ ∞ ♥

At the start of this day;

2 companions & I decided to walk a way;

So down the lane we went side by side;

An adventure to find was our only guide;

With sky as our ceiling & earth as our floor;

Leaving our prints as traces for others to see where we journey once more.

Just as day turns to night each beginning has an end;

But in truth, is it gone or like the river just disappearing around the bend;

For after darkness comes, the light showing what the shadows hold;

Continuing on lifes' journey experiencing beauty as it begins to unfold.

∞♥∞♥∞♥∞♥∞♥∞♥∞♥∞♥∞♥∞♥∞♥∞♥∞♥∞♥∞♥∞♥∞♥

If tempted to do something, not terrible, but not good;

Yet leaving its' own traces, will it be understood;

Upon fulfilling this temptation, doing this "thing";

Freewill has its' own bite, it carries its' own sting;

Choices that are made carry repercussions, like ripples or waves they move out;

Centering within, vibrations of the soul with every song it shall sing, of that there is no doubt.

∞♥∞♥∞♥∞♥∞♥∞♥∞♥∞♥∞♥∞♥∞♥∞♥∞♥∞♥∞♥∞♥∞♥

Thoughts run rampant within my mind;

As this journey I take for it is peace I wish to find;

Trying to harness the waves of thought in an ocean of time;

Only creating such ripples of energy that are pure & sublime.

∞ ♥ ∞ ♥ ∞ ♥ ∞ ♥ ∞ ♥ ∞ ♥ ∞ ♥ ∞ ♥ ∞ ♥ ∞ ♥ ∞ ♥ ∞ ♥ ∞ ♥ ∞ ♥ ∞ ♥ ∞ ♥ ∞ ♥

There is much to do & see in this world that we share;

Through the magic of words, expression of such is the task that I dare;

Difficulty includes our unique perception of all that we think we see;

For the moment it takes for me to stand exactly where you were, everything is different in what is now in front of me.

∞ ♥ ∞ ♥ ∞ ♥ ∞ ♥ ∞ ♥ ∞ ♥ ∞ ♥ ∞ ♥ ∞ ♥ ∞ ♥ ∞ ♥ ∞ ♥ ∞ ♥ ∞ ♥ ∞ ♥ ∞ ♥ ∞ ♥

My thoughts are of you & so much I wish to say;

Looking through old writings, searching for words written prior to this day;

Seeing so much meant for only you;

An email I send at this days end simply stating, "☹ I miss you."

∞ ♥ ∞ ♥ ∞ ♥ ∞ ♥ ∞ ♥ ∞ ♥ ∞ ♥ ∞ ♥ ∞ ♥ ∞ ♥ ∞ ♥ ∞ ♥ ∞ ♥ ∞ ♥ ∞ ♥ ∞ ♥ ∞ ♥

Many people upon my soul have left traces;

This journey has allowed me to look upon many faces;

Others I have not met as they have already gone;

If you listen closely you can hear they still sing a very sweet song.

∞ ♥ ∞ ♥ ∞ ♥ ∞ ♥ ∞ ♥ ∞ ♥ ∞ ♥ ∞ ♥ ∞ ♥ ∞ ♥ ∞ ♥ ∞ ♥ ∞ ♥ ∞ ♥ ∞ ♥ ∞ ♥

There are many gifts in life, given each day;

If one shall only take the opportunity that has come their way;

Life is full of chance, full of risk it is true;

I believe there to be moments of Fate but always the choice is up to you.

∞ ♥ ∞ ♥ ∞ ♥ ∞ ♥ ∞ ♥ ∞ ♥ ∞ ♥ ∞ ♥ ∞ ♥ ∞ ♥ ∞ ♥ ∞ ♥ ∞ ♥ ∞ ♥ ∞ ♥ ∞ ♥

If your life was a book, within its' pages what would you see;

Colorful rainbows, sunrises, sunsets, thunderstorms, love & happiness, sorrow & despair, what story would your words tell me;

Would you describe a beautiful autumn morning with grass that is green slowly turning brown;

Trees with their leaves that now float to the ground;

A sky so blue while filled with the suns' brilliant white light;

Getting a glimpse of your breath in the cool morning air, listening to birds near & far . . . Everything in life bringing you delight;

Would you share your hopes & dreams & wishes that you hold within your heart & long to have come true;

Would the pages in your book include thoughts of me as do the pages in mine include the thoughts of love I hold for you.

∞ ♥ ∞ ♥ ∞ ♥ ∞ ♥ ∞ ♥ ∞ ♥ ∞ ♥ ∞ ♥ ∞ ♥ ∞ ♥ ∞ ♥ ∞ ♥ ∞ ♥ ∞ ♥ ∞ ♥ ∞ ♥

A life lived in passion is a life lived in love;
A life lived to the fullest surrounded by light from above.

A Fathers' Love

"My child come to me, find comfort in my arms while laying your head upon my chest";

"Listen to the beat of my heart, feel safe & secure while you have a much needed rest";

"Your journey has been long filled with joys & sorrows, long days & nights, yet there is so much more awaiting you & much more in this life that you are meant to do";

"My child, no matter where you are, I hold you within my heart & I am always with you".

∞♥∞♥∞♥∞♥∞♥∞♥∞♥∞♥∞♥∞♥∞♥∞♥∞♥∞♥∞♥∞♥

Sunlight dances on the water, as do a few remaining leaves on the trees;
Feeling a chill upon my skin, receiving a kiss from the cool morning breeze;
Within nature I can let everything go allowing myself to be at ease.

∞♥∞♥∞♥∞♥∞♥∞♥∞♥∞♥∞♥∞♥∞♥∞♥∞♥∞♥∞♥∞♥

May your future be bright;

May your memories be of happier days untold;

May you behold beauty within your sight;

May you be filled with love as the days & years before you unfold.

∞ ♥ ∞ ♥ ∞ ♥ ∞ ♥ ∞ ♥ ∞ ♥ ∞ ♥ ∞ ♥ ∞ ♥ ∞ ♥ ∞ ♥ ∞ ♥ ∞ ♥ ∞ ♥ ∞ ♥ ∞ ♥

Ready for battle, now standing in a Warriors' stance;

For what is right in truth prepared to engage in the Warriors' dance;

Armor in place & blade in hand;

Target revealed & in my sight determining where the blow may land;

Only truth from thy lips, only truth may reach my ear;

For it is truth that protects all, setting all free as there is nothing to fear.

∞ ♥ ∞ ♥ ∞ ♥ ∞ ♥ ∞ ♥ ∞ ♥ ∞ ♥ ∞ ♥ ∞ ♥ ∞ ♥ ∞ ♥ ∞ ♥ ∞ ♥ ∞ ♥ ∞ ♥ ∞ ♥

Within the stillness, silence is everywhere;

Absence of movement upon the earth as well as in the air;

Peaceful tranquility, love, lingers there;

Within the stillness, the silence that is everywhere.

∞ ♥ ∞ ♥ ∞ ♥ ∞ ♥ ∞ ♥ ∞ ♥ ∞ ♥ ∞ ♥ ∞ ♥ ∞ ♥ ∞ ♥ ∞ ♥ ∞ ♥ ∞ ♥ ∞ ♥ ∞ ♥

So much I wish to do, so much I wish to see;

There is a quest calling from within, I feel as if there is a journey in front of me;

Distant lands, they beckon, like a siren calls men to the sea;

Traditions & knowledge, left for me to find, of a people who walked this earth long before me.

∞ ♥ ∞ ♥ ∞ ♥ ∞ ♥ ∞ ♥ ∞ ♥ ∞ ♥ ∞ ♥ ∞ ♥ ∞ ♥ ∞ ♥ ∞ ♥ ∞ ♥ ∞ ♥ ∞ ♥ ∞ ♥

Treasures found upon a quest;

Understanding of truth the ultimate test;

Secrets revealed within messages received;

When in truth we live, we cannot be deceived.

∞ ♥ ∞ ♥ ∞ ♥ ∞ ♥ ∞ ♥ ∞ ♥ ∞ ♥ ∞ ♥ ∞ ♥ ∞ ♥ ∞ ♥ ∞ ♥ ∞ ♥ ∞ ♥ ∞ ♥ ∞ ♥

I feel my heart beat so strong, so clear;

As if anothers' in rhythm with my own while near;

Two hearts as one, in sync for a time;

In love, there are no mistakes, only reason to match the rhyme.

∞ ♥ ∞ ♥ ∞ ♥ ∞ ♥ ∞ ♥ ∞ ♥ ∞ ♥ ∞ ♥ ∞ ♥ ∞ ♥ ∞ ♥ ∞ ♥ ∞ ♥ ∞ ♥ ∞ ♥ ∞ ♥

Sunshine or rainbows, blue skies or grey;
Time to work while leaving time to play;
Blessings received, promises fulfilled by the end of the day.

Laughter is so much sweeter after tears.

∞ ♥ ∞ ♥ ∞ ♥ ∞ ♥ ∞ ♥ ∞ ♥ ∞ ♥ ∞ ♥ ∞ ♥ ∞ ♥ ∞ ♥ ∞ ♥ ∞ ♥ ∞ ♥ ∞ ♥ ∞ ♥ ∞ ♥

So many blessings in life, all the treasures it holds;
Each day a gift as before me it now unfolds;
May your joys be many & your sorrows be few;
Know that love through prayers & thoughts are sent to you.

∞ ♥ ∞ ♥ ∞ ♥ ∞ ♥ ∞ ♥ ∞ ♥ ∞ ♥ ∞ ♥ ∞ ♥ ∞ ♥ ∞ ♥ ∞ ♥ ∞ ♥ ∞ ♥ ∞ ♥ ∞ ♥ ∞ ♥

It is time to say "Goodbye", it is time to let you go;
I pray you know of the love I hold for you, truly it is more than you know;
Blessed be in your todays & tomorrows, love be with you wherever you go.

∞ ♥ ∞ ♥ ∞ ♥ ∞ ♥ ∞ ♥ ∞ ♥ ∞ ♥ ∞ ♥ ∞ ♥ ∞ ♥ ∞ ♥ ∞ ♥ ∞ ♥ ∞ ♥ ∞ ♥ ∞ ♥ ∞ ♥

Stars of the night in the heavens above;
Moon shining bright leading me home to the ones I love.

∞ ♥ ∞ ♥ ∞ ♥ ∞ ♥ ∞ ♥ ∞ ♥ ∞ ♥ ∞ ♥ ∞ ♥ ∞ ♥ ∞ ♥ ∞ ♥ ∞ ♥ ∞ ♥ ∞ ♥ ∞ ♥

Daybreak the beauty of the sun, it kisses the morning skies;
Grateful for all in creation as it appears before my eyes.

∞ ♥ ∞ ♥ ∞ ♥ ∞ ♥ ∞ ♥ ∞ ♥ ∞ ♥ ∞ ♥ ∞ ♥ ∞ ♥ ∞ ♥ ∞ ♥ ∞ ♥ ∞ ♥ ∞ ♥ ∞ ♥

Greet each day with a smile & a song;
Listen to the rhythm of your heart as you journey along;
Keeping all your intentions pure & true;
Blessings in life will find their way to you.

∞ ♥ ∞ ♥ ∞ ♥ ∞ ♥ ∞ ♥ ∞ ♥ ∞ ♥ ∞ ♥ ∞ ♥ ∞ ♥ ∞ ♥ ∞ ♥ ∞ ♥ ∞ ♥ ∞ ♥ ∞ ♥

With each ending comes a new beginning.

∞ ♥ ∞ ♥ ∞ ♥ ∞ ♥ ∞ ♥ ∞ ♥ ∞ ♥ ∞ ♥ ∞ ♥ ∞ ♥ ∞ ♥ ∞ ♥ ∞ ♥ ∞ ♥ ∞ ♥ ∞ ♥

A few friends got together for a weekend reprieve;

Much needed break from responsibilities for us all, I believe;

Grateful for great friends, good food & good fun;

Even more grateful for home & loved ones to whom I return when my day is done.

∞ ♥ ∞ ♥ ∞ ♥ ∞ ♥ ∞ ♥ ∞ ♥ ∞ ♥ ∞ ♥ ∞ ♥ ∞ ♥ ∞ ♥ ∞ ♥ ∞ ♥ ∞ ♥ ∞ ♥ ∞ ♥ ∞ ♥

At first when I looked upon the river, it appeared to have a thin sheet of ice;

Not wanting to believe what I saw, I thought I had better look at it twice;

Life sometimes appears as one thing when in actuality it is not;

And with taking a better look we find we are better off now then what we first thought.

∞ ♥ ∞ ♥ ∞ ♥ ∞ ♥ ∞ ♥ ∞ ♥ ∞ ♥ ∞ ♥ ∞ ♥ ∞ ♥ ∞ ♥ ∞ ♥ ∞ ♥ ∞ ♥ ∞ ♥ ∞ ♥ ∞ ♥

A call from an Angel, the connection made by phone;

Gods' gentle way of reminding me we do not have to deal with life all alone;

Others will watch over us, as with all blessings, these earth Angels will be made known.

∞ ♥ ∞ ♥ ∞ ♥ ∞ ♥ ∞ ♥ ∞ ♥ ∞ ♥ ∞ ♥ ∞ ♥ ∞ ♥ ∞ ♥ ∞ ♥ ∞ ♥ ∞ ♥ ∞ ♥ ∞ ♥ ∞ ♥

As sunlight glistens on the water thoughts dance through my mind;

When we allow it peace & contentment in life we may find;

So many blessings & gifts await us as we continue this life to explore;

Trusting always we receive exactly what we need yet to find we are blessed with much more.

∞♥∞♥∞♥∞♥∞♥∞♥∞♥∞♥∞♥∞♥∞♥∞♥∞♥∞♥∞♥∞♥∞♥

If given the choice to change moments in your life, what would it or they be?

For me, I would not, by changing just one moment then, today I would not be the same me;

By not falling in love I wouldn't have experienced a broken heart, so I could never know a love that is true;

By not taking chances in lifes' adventures I would probably have fewer scars, but maybe I would not have met you.

∞♥∞♥∞♥∞♥∞♥∞♥∞♥∞♥∞♥∞♥∞♥∞♥∞♥∞♥∞♥∞♥

A beautiful new day has arrived;

Sunshine & rainbows greet me as I open my eyes;

Simplicity in nature makes me grateful to be alive;

Natural beauty of this world there is no disguise.

∞♥∞♥∞♥∞♥∞♥∞♥∞♥∞♥∞♥∞♥∞♥∞♥∞♥∞♥∞♥∞♥

I seek & find the one who best honors the needs of my soul;

One created from two, equals who complete each other in balance

making each separate yet whole;

Blessed to find a love pure & true;

Blessed to know love that is held within you;

My heart you hold within your hand;

Through space & time forever side by side to stand.

Happy Birthday, dear friend, on Halloween;

I believe more treats than tricks for you this day shall be seen;

You are a blessing placed among many upon this earth;

I celebrate today with you, your day of birth! ☺

Tyler's Tricky Treat

A year ago these plans were made;

So upon the counter the ingredients were laid;

Around Tyler's waist, Auntie's apron I did tie;

That is when I first caught the Impish grin with my eye;

Within the kitchen, a mess or two we made while in Halloween's Spirit we created our own witch's brew;

We poured & we stirred all being done with the magic of laughter & love, part of our gift for you;

Everything turned out as planned as we did mix & measure;

Although I believe I received the greatest gift, for this love & laughter creating memories I shall always treasure; ☺

Knowing a Grandma can magically find a way for a 7 year olds expectations to meet;

Making her dreams come true while creating Tyler's Tricky Treat.

I know it is Faith that fuels my dreams;

A whisper of Hope lives within, or so it seems.

The levels at which I feel I do not know if I can explain;
With an inner knowing the intensity of happiness balances the intensity
of pain.

Allowing the light of love to guide the way;
Shadows within begin to become less fearsome each new day;
Others are near who have walked a similar path in life;
Call upon them, when things seem too dark, when feeling overwhelmed
with strife;
Sages who have walked this earth before;
Have much to share & are willing companions, one must only open
the door.

True love is when you love someone's soul—heart—body & mind

∞ ♥ ∞ ♥ ∞ ♥ ∞ ♥ ∞ ♥ ∞ ♥ ∞ ♥ ∞ ♥ ∞ ♥ ∞ ♥ ∞ ♥ ∞ ♥ ∞ ♥ ∞ ♥ ∞ ♥

There is much within me, I have yet to understand;
Each day I change as I travel upon this land;
At times my only companion is my shadow that I see;
But within the light, even it no longer travels with me;
Many steps upon this earth I seemingly have traveled alone;
That is when I find the greatest lessons in life I am shown;
Many surround us with love with each new step, each & every stride;
Truth reveals all, in love & light, nothing may hide.

∞ ♥ ∞ ♥ ∞ ♥ ∞ ♥ ∞ ♥ ∞ ♥ ∞ ♥ ∞ ♥ ∞ ♥ ∞ ♥ ∞ ♥ ∞ ♥ ∞ ♥ ∞ ♥ ∞ ♥ ∞ ♥

Happy Birthday to you, dear Lee;
A day of joy & happiness before you, I see;
As you are surrounded with family & friends, love to you they bring;
Across the miles, I will join in, Happy Birthday to you, I also sing.

∞ ♥ ∞ ♥ ∞ ♥ ∞ ♥ ∞ ♥ ∞ ♥ ∞ ♥ ∞ ♥ ∞ ♥ ∞ ♥ ∞ ♥ ∞ ♥ ∞ ♥ ∞ ♥ ∞ ♥ ∞ ♥

It is the simple things in life I find I truly love;

Sunshine on the water, a kiss from my dog, or listening to the song of a dove;

There is a stillness, a quiet that fills this morning, the beginning to a beautiful day;

Grateful for the blessings, great & small, for everyone & everything that is sent my way.

∞ ♥ ∞ ♥ ∞ ♥ ∞ ♥ ∞ ♥ ∞ ♥ ∞ ♥ ∞ ♥ ∞ ♥ ∞ ♥ ∞ ♥ ∞ ♥ ∞ ♥ ∞ ♥ ∞ ♥ ∞ ♥

The wisdom of sages more & more I find;

Like pieces of a puzzle they come together in my mind;

Living life is like weaving a tapestry created by our own freewill;

Each thought, each action becoming a thread having a place to fill.

∞ ♥ ∞ ♥ ∞ ♥ ∞ ♥ ∞ ♥ ∞ ♥ ∞ ♥ ∞ ♥ ∞ ♥ ∞ ♥ ∞ ♥ ∞ ♥ ∞ ♥ ∞ ♥ ∞ ♥ ∞ ♥

Thank you Father, for the blessings of your love that come my way;

My mind, heart & soul take flight like a Phoenix rises from the ashes with each new day;

Through your love, I see, hear, feel & know things I have come to understand;

Guided by you through all of my life, you are at my side, you continue to hold my hand.

There is much in life, each day we give & receive;
There is goodness in all with every beat of my heart I will continue to
believe.

∞ ♥ ∞ ♥ ∞ ♥ ∞ ♥ ∞ ♥ ∞ ♥ ∞ ♥ ∞ ♥ ∞ ♥ ∞ ♥ ∞ ♥ ∞ ♥ ∞ ♥ ∞ ♥ ∞ ♥ ∞ ♥

Some days, people or things seem darker than others, yet within all
there is light;
With each step taken, each word spoken, each thought, each chooses
wrong or right.

∞ ♥ ∞ ♥ ∞ ♥ ∞ ♥ ∞ ♥ ∞ ♥ ∞ ♥ ∞ ♥ ∞ ♥ ∞ ♥ ∞ ♥ ∞ ♥ ∞ ♥ ∞ ♥ ∞ ♥ ∞ ♥

In silence, my thoughts seem so natural & so profound;
In silence, I know all that I am & accept what I have found;
In silence, I walk, afraid if I speak, my voice shall send my thoughts
away;
In silence, I find my heart & soul have much to say;
In silence, I pray for myself & yet more so for many others where ever
they may be;
In silence, all my love is given freely to you from me.

∞ ♥ ∞ ♥ ∞ ♥ ∞ ♥ ∞ ♥ ∞ ♥ ∞ ♥ ∞ ♥ ∞ ♥ ∞ ♥ ∞ ♥ ∞ ♥ ∞ ♥ ∞ ♥ ∞ ♥ ∞ ♥

A day to remember all who have given of themselves to protect & serve
so many others;

In times of wars & peace giving for all they love, they are mothers,
fathers, sisters, brothers;

I & so many more say, "Thank you & blessed be for caring so much
for another."

The presence of a soul in ones' life is a gift freely given, not to be
controlled by another but out of choices each soul has made;

Whether husband, wife, friend or lover, a companion in life to walk the
path before you laid;

Freely give & freely take for without balance, acceptance & unconditional
love, a price shall surely be paid;

Take my hand & walk with me as long as you wish, together in love we
will continue on with no need to be afraid;

Life is a blessing, teaching many lessons along the way, some hard,
some easy, but all are created by the choices each soul has freely made.

At times I have a feeling that is so strong;
A feeling that part of my heart is missing for far too long;
Come, fly with me forever & we can create our own magical song.

∞ ♥ ∞ ♥ ∞ ♥ ∞ ♥ ∞ ♥ ∞ ♥ ∞ ♥ ∞ ♥ ∞ ♥ ∞ ♥ ∞ ♥ ∞ ♥ ∞ ♥ ∞ ♥ ∞ ♥ ∞ ♥

M' lady Winters' first kiss, traces of her first visit she has left behind;
Soon I shall travel on magical adventures, mystical places within my mind;
Narnia shall surround me once again, its beauty I may constantly see;
Like a fire in the hearth at home, brings warmth & comfort, the fires
in the soul shall guide me.

∞ ♥ ∞ ♥ ∞ ♥ ∞ ♥ ∞ ♥ ∞ ♥ ∞ ♥ ∞ ♥ ∞ ♥ ∞ ♥ ∞ ♥ ∞ ♥ ∞ ♥ ∞ ♥ ∞ ♥ ∞ ♥

Winters' first kiss, traces left behind;
Pictures of its' beauty come flooding back & fill my mind;
I cannot help but wonder, what adventures & treasures winters' journey
will bring for me to find.

∞ ♥ ∞ ♥ ∞ ♥ ∞ ♥ ∞ ♥ ∞ ♥ ∞ ♥ ∞ ♥ ∞ ♥ ∞ ♥ ∞ ♥ ∞ ♥ ∞ ♥ ∞ ♥ ∞ ♥ ∞ ♥

Lifes' littlest gestures just might be lifes' greatest pleasures;
We must only be open to receive life's gifts thereby increasing our own
treasures.

∞ ♥ ∞ ♥ ∞ ♥ ∞ ♥ ∞ ♥ ∞ ♥ ∞ ♥ ∞ ♥ ∞ ♥ ∞ ♥ ∞ ♥ ∞ ♥ ∞ ♥ ∞ ♥ ∞ ♥

Everywhere I look I see your grace;
I feel your love that transcends time & space;
Your gentleness somehow caresses my face;
Always grateful you are but a thought away, any time, any place.

∞ ♥ ∞ ♥ ∞ ♥ ∞ ♥ ∞ ♥ ∞ ♥ ∞ ♥ ∞ ♥ ∞ ♥ ∞ ♥ ∞ ♥ ∞ ♥ ∞ ♥ ∞ ♥ ∞ ♥

Blade in hand, fire in my eyes;
No place to run, no place to hide;
I know where you are from my place in the skies.

∞ ♥ ∞ ♥ ∞ ♥ ∞ ♥ ∞ ♥ ∞ ♥ ∞ ♥ ∞ ♥ ∞ ♥ ∞ ♥ ∞ ♥ ∞ ♥ ∞ ♥ ∞ ♥ ∞ ♥

Today is your day, we celebrate your birth;

Blessed by you & your adventurous spirit here on earth;

May each day bring to you happiness never before known;

Love & kindness returned to you greater than the love you have shown;

May the desires of your heart & your dreams come true;

Many happy birthday wishes from me to you.

Last night I had an emptiness that filled my soul;

I cried as that emptiness had taken its' toll;

I prayed to be able to sleep in my Fathers' arms;

And to be protected by the Angels from all harms.

∞ ♥ ∞ ♥ ∞ ♥ ∞ ♥ ∞ ♥ ∞ ♥ ∞ ♥ ∞ ♥ ∞ ♥ ∞ ♥ ∞ ♥ ∞ ♥ ∞ ♥ ∞ ♥ ∞ ♥ ∞ ♥

An overcast, cool somewhat dreary day;
A wet fog lingers, yet within peace is here to stay;
The river itself calm & slow, the color of jade I am shown;
A breeze across the tops of the leafless trees is gently blown;
With every season there is such beauty to be found;
When one looks carefully there are blessings all around.

Within my heart, I shall not carry your guilt or your shame;
Within my mind, I shall not take on that for which I am not to blame;
Each choice you make is yours, & yours alone;
Just as I am responsible & accountable for the choices that are my own;
Life is too short for deceit, being sucked into a game;
I will continue to love you & accept you for who you are just the same.

∞ ♥ ∞ ♥ ∞ ♥ ∞ ♥ ∞ ♥ ∞ ♥ ∞ ♥ ∞ ♥ ∞ ♥ ∞ ♥ ∞ ♥ ∞ ♥ ∞ ♥ ∞ ♥ ∞ ♥ ∞ ♥

There are times in my life when I have felt totally alone,
yet those same times I have always felt the most loved.

∞ ♥ ∞ ♥ ∞ ♥ ∞ ♥ ∞ ♥ ∞ ♥ ∞ ♥ ∞ ♥ ∞ ♥ ∞ ♥ ∞ ♥ ∞ ♥ ∞ ♥ ∞ ♥ ∞ ♥ ∞ ♥

A day of Thanksgiving, a national holiday;
A day to show our gratitude for every blessing that comes our way;
A day of understanding & acceptance all is exactly as it is meant to be;
A day to share a love for life & heart felt gratitude for blessings past & present as well as for the future held for you & me.

∞ ♥ ∞ ♥ ∞ ♥ ∞ ♥ ∞ ♥ ∞ ♥ ∞ ♥ ∞ ♥ ∞ ♥ ∞ ♥ ∞ ♥ ∞ ♥ ∞ ♥ ∞ ♥ ∞ ♥ ∞ ♥

There is contentment within such as it is before I have not known;
It is as if somehow deep inside, I understand, everything is as it should be & I am exactly where I belong;
The world continues to change around me yet everyday blessings I am shown.

∞ ♥ ∞ ♥ ∞ ♥ ∞ ♥ ∞ ♥ ∞ ♥ ∞ ♥ ∞ ♥ ∞ ♥ ∞ ♥ ∞ ♥ ∞ ♥ ∞ ♥ ∞ ♥ ∞ ♥ ∞ ♥

Feel the beat of my heart . . . Hear the thoughts within my mind;
Do that which is right . . . Much joy & happiness you shall find.

∞ ♥ ∞ ♥ ∞ ♥ ∞ ♥ ∞ ♥ ∞ ♥ ∞ ♥ ∞ ♥ ∞ ♥ ∞ ♥ ∞ ♥ ∞ ♥ ∞ ♥ ∞ ♥ ∞ ♥ ∞ ♥

I Am Grateful . . . For The Blessings . . .

I am eternally grateful for all that I see;
For the blessings of a rainbow given from thee;
I am grateful for the dreams from within myself;
For the blessings of living them, not placing them on a shelf;
I am grateful for the shadows & the light that fills each day;
For the blessings of the shadows, the light grows brighter while lighting my way;
I am grateful for the depth of my heart with which I feel others so much;
For the blessings of their every thought, word, or deed, I feel the energy of their touch;
I am grateful for all that is held within me, in mind, body, heart & soul allowing all of me to dance & sing;
For the blessings of life each one, like a droplet of water creating ripples continuing to all, a gift through love to bring;
I am grateful for the fires that burn, creating love within;
For the blessings of leaving no room for hatred or angers' roots to begin;
I am grateful to know, all in creation is filled with your light;
For the blessings of acceptance for all choices through freewill with the best ones revealing a future that is bright;
I am grateful for knowing my own adventurous spirit, having the strength & courage to spread my wings, climb to new heights & soar;
For the blessings to see beyond the mundane to such beauty held in all life, creating a desire for more;
I am grateful for each & every soul that has been, is or will be in my life, whether they remain now on earth or are in the heavens above;
For the blessings they have all touched my life, my mind, my heart, my soul, leaving forever upon me, within me an imprint of their love.

Like a Phoenix out of the ashes, my soul does rise;
Like a Dragon in flight, my spirit soars to the skies;
Like a Master of magic, I create & live my own destiny, changing fate;
Like a Gypsy traveling, for my next journey I can hardly wait.

∞ ♥ ∞ ♥ ∞ ♥ ∞ ♥ ∞ ♥ ∞ ♥ ∞ ♥ ∞ ♥ ∞ ♥ ∞ ♥ ∞ ♥ ∞ ♥ ∞ ♥ ∞ ♥ ∞ ♥ ∞ ♥

May faith keep you strong, knowing our Father is by your side;
May His Angels surround you with much love & light, healing you,
mind body & soul always there to be your guide;
May the prayers of the many hold you close every moment of every day;
May you feel the love of others sent to you whether they are close or
far away.

∞ ♥ ∞ ♥ ∞ ♥ ∞ ♥ ∞ ♥ ∞ ♥ ∞ ♥ ∞ ♥ ∞ ♥ ∞ ♥ ∞ ♥ ∞ ♥ ∞ ♥ ∞ ♥ ∞ ♥ ∞ ♥

The color Red, the color of passion & fire;
The color Red, the color of words within it does inspire;
The color Red, the color of anger, of rage;
The color Red, the color of love as your heart sets the stage.

∞ ♥ ∞ ♥ ∞ ♥ ∞ ♥ ∞ ♥ ∞ ♥ ∞ ♥ ∞ ♥ ∞ ♥ ∞ ♥ ∞ ♥ ∞ ♥ ∞ ♥ ∞ ♥ ∞ ♥ ∞ ♥

As I watch the sunrise because I cannot sleep;
I wonder what adventures this day does hold;
With the passion within me, the secrets my heart does keep;
I shall open the door to receive many treasures untold.

Thoughts for the Mind;
To touch the Heart;
Gifts of the Soul

I hold all in life near & dear to my heart;
A love for all of creation that shall never part.

Merry Christmas to one & all, family & friends;

May you be blessed with love, genuine & true that never ends;

May you be blessed with happiness & good cheer;

May you be blessed with heartfelt memories as you reflect upon the past year.

As 2010 now reaches its' end;

My warmest regards from my heart, I to thee send;

A time for reflection on the years' events has come at last;

A time to cherish some memories as we look upon the past;

With the New Year comes new beginnings, new adventures are at hand;

A time to achieve dreams, reach for new goals, live life as planned;

As always we shall have choices to make along the way;

To walk the path before us or perhaps simply do nothing & stay;

In honor of your own freewill, I will not mold you into something I wish to see;

I can only accept you as you are, as the soul you are meant to be;

I shall continue to hold no expectations of you, thereby no disappointment shall I find;

But I shall love you always hopefully touching your heart, soul & mind;

Please do not be disappointed when I do not let you mold me;

My wings you may not clip, for my spirit / my soul is to remain wild, untamed & free.

I sit in silence to start my day;

The words from my heart in my mind I pray;

Allowing me to send any sorrows away;

I place myself in your loving hands, so come what may;

In love & light I shall make it through another day.

∞ ♥ ∞ ♥ ∞ ♥ ∞ ♥ ∞ ♥ ∞ ♥ ∞ ♥ ∞ ♥ ∞ ♥ ∞ ♥ ∞ ♥ ∞ ♥ ∞ ♥ ∞ ♥ ∞ ♥ ∞ ♥ ∞ ♥

My hair has grayed, my body has many scars;

My feet continue to walk this earth, my head & heart reach for the stars.

∞ ♥ ∞ ♥ ∞ ♥ ∞ ♥ ∞ ♥ ∞ ♥ ∞ ♥ ∞ ♥ ∞ ♥ ∞ ♥ ∞ ♥ ∞ ♥ ∞ ♥ ∞ ♥ ∞ ♥ ∞ ♥ ∞ ♥

May you be blessed with much love & happiness all your days;

May you see the treasures of the rainbows when life's rains go away;

May you find the magic held within this world, this life & know all that is good is here to stay;

I pray you find the beauty in living each day . . .

∞ ♥ ∞ ♥ ∞ ♥ ∞ ♥ ∞ ♥ ∞ ♥ ∞ ♥ ∞ ♥ ∞ ♥ ∞ ♥ ∞ ♥ ∞ ♥ ∞ ♥ ∞ ♥ ∞ ♥ ∞ ♥ ∞ ♥

Whispers, sweet, I hear within my head;

A longing within to look outside, to gaze upon a moonlit night my eyes are led;

A love fills me inside like a beautiful radiating light;

I knowingly hold the key that unlocks the magic of this world whether it be day or night;

I shall reveal all that I am, becoming an open book;

There is much more to me then meets the eye, gaze upon my soul & take a deeper look.

There are times I feel so alone;

Times life is exactly as it is meant to be;

Times I wonder if when you look at me, is it my soul you truly see;

Alone with my thoughts that are mine . . . & mine alone.

Look into my eyes if it is truly me, you wish to know;

They reveal much, the depth of my heart & the way to see my soul,
they to you will show;

There you shall see laughter & joy as well as heartache & pain;

They reveal all, as I have nothing to lose & you have everything to gain;

My eyes are the windows to my soul, take the journey if it is a place
you dare to go;

Look into my eyes if it is truly me, you wish to know.

Grateful for such beauty before me that which I have not seen seemingly
for so long;

A new day begun, my head no longer clouded allowing me now to sing
my souls' sweet song;

For a time feeling out of place, out of balance, but through diligence &
faith I am right where I belong;

My heart beats again with a rhythm all its' own, a rhythm that is steady
& strong.

Love is the one thing we instinctively believe in;
The one thing that is with us from the moment this life we begin;
Love is the one thing through all seasons of life that does remain;
The one thing forever constant in life it shall reign.

∞ ♥ ∞ ♥ ∞ ♥ ∞ ♥ ∞ ♥ ∞ ♥ ∞ ♥ ∞ ♥ ∞ ♥ ∞ ♥ ∞ ♥ ∞ ♥ ∞ ♥ ∞ ♥ ∞ ♥

I shall continue to cherish each memory held in the past;
I shall continue to dream of the promises held in the future;
I shall continue to live each moment to it's fullest, as the gift it is meant to be, in the present.

∞ ♥ ∞ ♥ ∞ ♥ ∞ ♥ ∞ ♥ ∞ ♥ ∞ ♥ ∞ ♥ ∞ ♥ ∞ ♥ ∞ ♥ ∞ ♥ ∞ ♥ ∞ ♥ ∞ ♥

Behind blue eyes can you see the truth of me;
Or do you see only that which you wish to see;
Behind blue eyes there is so much more;
Look deep within, perhaps you shall find that which you are looking for;
Behind blue eyes, I am certain there shall be revealed more than you wish to see;
Can you accept the truth of who I am meant to be . . . ME.

∞ ♥ ∞ ♥ ∞ ♥ ∞ ♥ ∞ ♥ ∞ ♥ ∞ ♥ ∞ ♥ ∞ ♥ ∞ ♥ ∞ ♥ ∞ ♥ ∞ ♥ ∞ ♥ ∞ ♥

I love you! And I miss you!

I am grateful for the time we shared . . . And although your body may
be gone, your love remains within my heart;

I am grateful to know that it is the love from which we never part.

∞ ♥ ∞ ♥ ∞ ♥ ∞ ♥ ∞ ♥ ∞ ♥ ∞ ♥ ∞ ♥ ∞ ♥ ∞ ♥ ∞ ♥ ∞ ♥ ∞ ♥ ∞ ♥ ∞ ♥ ∞ ♥

Feeling health within the body, brings forth a wealth held within the
mind;

A sense of balance within all of life is the blessing one may find;

Realizing ones' blessings in life, breathtaking moments, each being one
of a kind.

∞ ♥ ∞ ♥ ∞ ♥ ∞ ♥ ∞ ♥ ∞ ♥ ∞ ♥ ∞ ♥ ∞ ♥ ∞ ♥ ∞ ♥ ∞ ♥ ∞ ♥ ∞ ♥ ∞ ♥ ∞ ♥

Blessed be on this beautiful day;

May sunshine & laughter come your way;

Finding a heart filled with love forever to stay;

Blessed be on this beautiful day.

∞ ♥ ∞ ♥ ∞ ♥ ∞ ♥ ∞ ♥ ∞ ♥ ∞ ♥ ∞ ♥ ∞ ♥ ∞ ♥ ∞ ♥ ∞ ♥ ∞ ♥ ∞ ♥ ∞ ♥ ∞ ♥

The river now brown, no longer the color of jade;

A transformation overnight this beautiful river has made;

But with grey skies above & a river now brown;

The grass looks lush & greener a new wonder I have found;

Amazed at the beauty I have found upon this earth;

Yet more wondrous still, this seems to have been so from the moment of my birth;

Like the muddied waters of the river, words swirl within my mind;

Yet with paper & pen in hand, somehow it makes sense & clarity I find.

My two companions now outside, one gives their warning to the north the other gives hers' to the south;

As I gaze upon them, sensing their care & love for me, a gentle smile creeps across my mouth;

A Turkey sends out its greeting while hidden somewhere in the trees;

I watch as a King fisher catches breakfast across the muddy river as I stand in the light morning breeze;

My eyes gaze in awe & wonder as I take it all in, North, East & South;

And without thought or warning "Blessed Be" are the only words which escape from my mouth. ☺

My thoughts are drawn to you in so many ways;

They fill my mind throughout my nights, my days;

I am conflicted at times with which direction to go;

Filled with Faith I will follow my heart & go the right way I know;

I feel your thoughts of me & believe you feel mine of you;

A fire burns deep within me started so long ago it is true;

There is a magic in this life filled with destiny & fate;

For the one I seek & find, my heart, mind & soul tell me to wait;

To be with my equal in everyway, mind, body & soul;

As two become one, as pars coming together makes us a whole.

∞ ♥ ∞ ♥ ∞ ♥ ∞ ♥ ∞ ♥ ∞ ♥ ∞ ♥ ∞ ♥ ∞ ♥ ∞ ♥ ∞ ♥ ∞ ♥ ∞ ♥ ∞ ♥ ∞ ♥ ∞ ♥ ∞ ♥

If I died tomorrow, of myself, what can I say;

I believe I tried my best each & every day

That I learned about loving unconditionally;

I knowingly felt love from others given to me;

That I looked at all my life, like looking through the eyes of a child;

I lived my life to the fullest, respectfully & yet at times a bit wild;

That the passion I held for life could make my gray skies turn blue;

I held a love for myself which allowed me to love others & all in life,

honestly & true.

∞ ♥ ∞ ♥ ∞ ♥ ∞ ♥ ∞ ♥ ∞ ♥ ∞ ♥ ∞ ♥ ∞ ♥ ∞ ♥ ∞ ♥ ∞ ♥ ∞ ♥ ∞ ♥ ∞ ♥ ∞ ♥

There is a magic to this world known throughout the ages, understood so long ago;

Yet today seemingly so few accept it & use it & continue to grow;

It has been said by the sages for days long past;

To understand lifes' truth, light upon the shadows we must cast;

Gifts of untold treasure lie within you & me;

With Love & Light we remove the darkness from us, allowing all, our true selves to see.

Some time ago a message had been given to me;

"Your future is in the past", all is as it is meant to be;

With Faith I continue to follow my heart where it leads, knowing all shall be revealed;

Lifes' path as I walk in truth, blessings of love unconcealed.

∞ ♥ ∞ ♥ ∞ ♥ ∞ ♥ ∞ ♥ ∞ ♥ ∞ ♥ ∞ ♥ ∞ ♥ ∞ ♥ ∞ ♥ ∞ ♥ ∞ ♥ ∞ ♥ ∞ ♥ ∞ ♥

Sometimes, I have been truly amazed by my own thoughts, my perception of life or life situations. I would admit I truly love my life today. It still has its' ups & downs, more up than down, at least the way I see things. I also prefer the concept of people being in my life because they freely choose to . . . We cannot "own" anything or anyone other than ourselves. We are responsible for our own happiness; no one else can make us happy . . . We can feel happiness due to someone's presence but nothing they do can actually make us happy.

∞ ♥ ∞ ♥ ∞ ♥ ∞ ♥ ∞ ♥ ∞ ♥ ∞ ♥ ∞ ♥ ∞ ♥ ∞ ♥ ∞ ♥ ∞ ♥ ∞ ♥ ∞ ♥ ∞ ♥

My heart, it aches, as my soul cries out, my voice is muted by my own hand;
My eyes grow teary as my mind sees my dreams, how I long for that day to come;
My heart leads the way, all of me to follow, for it is truly the only way I know to stand;
My path is long & at times weary, yet I know, I am not to travel it alone.

∞ ♥ ∞ ♥ ∞ ♥ ∞ ♥ ∞ ♥ ∞ ♥ ∞ ♥ ∞ ♥ ∞ ♥ ∞ ♥ ∞ ♥ ∞ ♥ ∞ ♥ ∞ ♥ ∞ ♥

There is a love in this world that is meant to be mine;
Without expectations there shall be no disappointments & truth shall not be denied;
A love so unconditional in every way to be in my life in its' own perfect time;
As choices are made that brings him to me for without him, my heart would have surely died.

∞ ♥ ∞ ♥ ∞ ♥ ∞ ♥ ∞ ♥ ∞ ♥ ∞ ♥ ∞ ♥ ∞ ♥ ∞ ♥ ∞ ♥ ∞ ♥ ∞ ♥ ∞ ♥ ∞ ♥

There are very few words to express how much love & adoration I have
for you;

Your accomplishments in life are a testament of the man you are with
only love shining through;

Each new day a blessing to have you in my life;

Through your examples, proving we may overcome so much, leaving
for us a beautiful love filled life.

∞ ♥ ∞ ♥ ∞ ♥ ∞ ♥ ∞ ♥ ∞ ♥ ∞ ♥ ∞ ♥ ∞ ♥ ∞ ♥ ∞ ♥ ∞ ♥ ∞ ♥ ∞ ♥ ∞ ♥ ∞ ♥ ∞ ♥

It has become abundantly clear your feelings for me;

The choice is yours as it always has been;

Unconditionally I will always love you, as it is meant t be;

Grateful for the truth I now know, with opened eyes I have seen.

(My child, I only wish you can see, feel & know the love I have for you!)

∞ ♥ ∞ ♥ ∞ ♥ ∞ ♥ ∞ ♥ ∞ ♥ ∞ ♥ ∞ ♥ ∞ ♥ ∞ ♥ ∞ ♥ ∞ ♥ ∞ ♥ ∞ ♥ ∞ ♥ ∞ ♥ ∞ ♥

To my family & friends both young & old, old & new;

I pray you are aware of the love I hold for you;

How grateful I am to have you in my life whether near or far;

You have blessed me beyond measure being exactly who you are;

I have no regrets living as I do;

I pray the same is true for you.

∞ ♥ ∞ ♥ ∞ ♥ ∞ ♥ ∞ ♥ ∞ ♥ ∞ ♥ ∞ ♥ ∞ ♥ ∞ ♥ ∞ ♥ ∞ ♥ ∞ ♥ ∞ ♥ ∞ ♥ ∞ ♥ ∞ ♥

Shine magnificent soul, shine like the stars above;

Shine, allowing the fire within to burn bright, as it is of love;

Shine, Little One, shine, being a light along the way;

Shine allowing all to see whether by night or by day.

My wish for you is to follow your heart;

Allowing it to lead you where you have been meant to be right from the start;

There are people, places & events in your life, all part of your fate;

Always at the perfect time never too soon, never too late.

I believe my life is continuously getting better every day;

I feel my dreams becoming my reality in every way;

I see many sign revealed that says love is here to stay;

I long for the moments with Him, always to remain safe I pray.

∞ ♥ ∞ ♥ ∞ ♥ ∞ ♥ ∞ ♥ ∞ ♥ ∞ ♥ ∞ ♥ ∞ ♥ ∞ ♥ ∞ ♥ ∞ ♥ ∞ ♥ ∞ ♥ ∞ ♥ ∞ ♥ ∞ ♥

My Sorcerer, you invade my dreams;

In the light of day or the darkness of night, it matters not or so it seems;

Like a Gypsy woman, I see many sights of you in a crystal ball;

The magic we share, I await your call;

Only in my dreams now I am at your side;

I long for you here & now as my reality, together having nothing to hide.

∞ ♥ ∞ ♥ ∞ ♥ ∞ ♥ ∞ ♥ ∞ ♥ ∞ ♥ ∞ ♥ ∞ ♥ ∞ ♥ ∞ ♥ ∞ ♥ ∞ ♥ ∞ ♥ ∞ ♥ ∞ ♥

I have followed my heart, its' emotions so real;

All I know now, is this heartache is what I feel;

A beautiful mid summers' day & I sit alone;

Choices have been made I accept the actions of my own;

Openly who I am I had to reveal;

That love is alive & passion is what I feel.

∞ ♥ ∞ ♥ ∞ ♥ ∞ ♥ ∞ ♥ ∞ ♥ ∞ ♥ ∞ ♥ ∞ ♥ ∞ ♥ ∞ ♥ ∞ ♥ ∞ ♥ ∞ ♥ ∞ ♥ ∞ ♥

With every beat of my heart I feel;

With every breath I take more becomes real.

∞ ♥ ∞ ♥ ∞ ♥ ∞ ♥ ∞ ♥ ∞ ♥ ∞ ♥ ∞ ♥ ∞ ♥ ∞ ♥ ∞ ♥ ∞ ♥ ∞ ♥ ∞ ♥ ∞ ♥ ∞ ♥

Dreams of you are what I see;

Believe & So it shall be;

I close my eyes & I see your face;

I pray within my heart, you know you have a special place;

Love transcends all, even time & space;

I long to be in your presence surrounded by your finery & grace.

As the sun begins to set in the western skies;

There is a fog in the meadows that has started to rise;

Something of love has touched his heart & soul of mine;

There is a peace & comfort that fills me, something sublime.

To my heart I understand I must always be true;

If I am not it will lead to a life of regrets;

So where my heart dos lead I will do what I must do.

∞ ♥ ∞ ♥ ∞ ♥ ∞ ♥ ∞ ♥ ∞ ♥ ∞ ♥ ∞ ♥ ∞ ♥ ∞ ♥ ∞ ♥ ∞ ♥ ∞ ♥ ∞ ♥ ∞ ♥ ∞ ♥

A moment outside under a moon brightly shining with a canopy of stars near by;

Looking to the western horizon there is Venus & the gentle glow of the Sun still kissing the sky;

The fog rises in the meadows just across the lane;

Reminded by such splendor within every moment in truth there is nothing to lose & everything to gain.

∞ ♥ ∞ ♥ ∞ ♥ ∞ ♥ ∞ ♥ ∞ ♥ ∞ ♥ ∞ ♥ ∞ ♥ ∞ ♥ ∞ ♥ ∞ ♥ ∞ ♥ ∞ ♥ ∞ ♥ ∞ ♥

While walking my chosen path I have found myself rather secluded. Making or at least trying to make, good choices, living life well while trying not to harm another. Having no guilt, no shame, and no regrets. A life of love & light. While so many willingly choose to do wrong to another or themselves, they are also surrounded by many, because like surrounds themselves with like . . . therefore, few walk my path. There is someone in this world that will walk by my side & love as my equal.

∞ ♥ ∞ ♥ ∞ ♥ ∞ ♥ ∞ ♥ ∞ ♥ ∞ ♥ ∞ ♥ ∞ ♥ ∞ ♥ ∞ ♥ ∞ ♥ ∞ ♥ ∞ ♥ ∞ ♥ ∞ ♥

Like an eagle in flight, I shall spread my wings & soar;

Taking in lifes' blessings as they are given I shall want nothing more.

∞ ♥ ∞ ♥ ∞ ♥ ∞ ♥ ∞ ♥ ∞ ♥ ∞ ♥ ∞ ♥ ∞ ♥ ∞ ♥ ∞ ♥ ∞ ♥ ∞ ♥ ∞ ♥ ∞ ♥ ∞ ♥

You continue to live your life as I continue to live mine;
I find I am at the mercy of the hands of time.

Choice

Having a choice of freewill or bondage;
I willingly choose freewill;
Having a choice of fire or ice;
I willingly choose fire;
Having a choice of honesty or lies;
I willingly choose honesty;
Having a choice of love or ill will;
I willingly choose love;
Having a choice of fulfillment or regret;
I willingly choose fulfillment;
Having a choice of acceptance or judgment;
I willingly choose acceptance;
Having a choice of walking on the narrow path or following
the multitude on the road;
I willingly choose walking the narrow path;
Having a choice of living surrounded by light or living surrounded by
darkness;
I willingly choose living surrounded by light.

∞ ♥ ∞ ♥ ∞ ♥ ∞ ♥ ∞ ♥ ∞ ♥ ∞ ♥ ∞ ♥ ∞ ♥ ∞ ♥ ∞ ♥ ∞ ♥ ∞ ♥ ∞ ♥ ∞ ♥

Believe & It Shall Be!

∞ ♥ ∞ ♥ ∞ ♥ ∞ ♥ ∞ ♥ ∞ ♥ ∞ ♥ ∞ ♥ ∞ ♥ ∞ ♥ ∞ ♥ ∞ ♥ ∞ ♥ ∞ ♥ ∞ ♥ ∞ ♥ ∞ ♥

With all of my heart, from the depths of my soul, I shall seek thee;
Through Faith, with my entire mind, I know all shall be as it is meant
to be.

∞ ♥ ∞ ♥ ∞ ♥ ∞ ♥ ∞ ♥ ∞ ♥ ∞ ♥ ∞ ♥ ∞ ♥ ∞ ♥ ∞ ♥ ∞ ♥ ∞ ♥ ∞ ♥ ∞ ♥ ∞ ♥ ∞ ♥

Knowing full well, that wishes & dreams come true;
Receiving that which is asked for, gifts or blessings given to you.

∞ ♥ ∞ ♥ ∞ ♥ ∞ ♥ ∞ ♥ ∞ ♥ ∞ ♥ ∞ ♥ ∞ ♥ ∞ ♥ ∞ ♥ ∞ ♥ ∞ ♥ ∞ ♥ ∞ ♥ ∞ ♥ ∞ ♥

If we get what we ask for, is it wise to turn away;
As if by magic your dreams do come true, blessings sent to you;
Requests sent from the heart to the heavens above;
Gifts given in answer, gifts given with unconditional love.

∞ ♥ ∞ ♥ ∞ ♥ ∞ ♥ ∞ ♥ ∞ ♥ ∞ ♥ ∞ ♥ ∞ ♥ ∞ ♥ ∞ ♥ ∞ ♥ ∞ ♥ ∞ ♥ ∞ ♥ ∞ ♥ ∞ ♥

My thoughts have turned to you on this cool summer night;
Sitting under the stars so familiar, memories that fill me with delight.

The world keeps spinning, just turning around;
Somehow my head is in the clouds while my feet are on the ground;
Life continues on in crazy yet simple way;
Realizing so much to be grateful for at the end of each day.

Do not turn your back on one who asks for help even if they have previously turned their back on you;
Give what you can, whole heartedly, the blessings of others shall come back in all you do.

∞ ♥ ∞ ♥ ∞ ♥ ∞ ♥ ∞ ♥ ∞ ♥ ∞ ♥ ∞ ♥ ∞ ♥ ∞ ♥ ∞ ♥ ∞ ♥ ∞ ♥ ∞ ♥ ∞ ♥

I thank you, for loving me, for holding me within your heart;
The truest of love, a love from which I never shall part;
To be held in your arms, a feeling that I am safe & secure;
I thank you for loving me, & teaching me of a love so genuine & pure.

∞ ♥ ∞ ♥ ∞ ♥ ∞ ♥ ∞ ♥ ∞ ♥ ∞ ♥ ∞ ♥ ∞ ♥ ∞ ♥ ∞ ♥ ∞ ♥ ∞ ♥ ∞ ♥ ∞ ♥ ∞ ♥

I thank you, for loving me, for holding me within your heart;
The truest of love, a love from which I never shall part;
To be held in your arms, a feeling that I safe & secure;
I thank you for loving me, & teaching me of a love so genuine & pure.

∞ ♥ ∞ ♥ ∞ ♥ ∞ ♥ ∞ ♥ ∞ ♥ ∞ ♥ ∞ ♥ ∞ ♥ ∞ ♥ ∞ ♥ ∞ ♥ ∞ ♥ ∞ ♥ ∞ ♥ ∞ ♥

Dragon's Flight . . . .
A personal journey of One mind, heart & soul.

∞ ♥ ∞ ♥ ∞ ♥ ∞ ♥ ∞ ♥ ∞ ♥ ∞ ♥ ∞ ♥ ∞ ♥ ∞ ♥ ∞ ♥ ∞ ♥ ∞ ♥ ∞ ♥ ∞ ♥ ∞ ♥

Some may say I have the heart of a fool;

But in reality, my heart is like a rare jewel;

My lifepath has taken me to wondrous places;

Able to look into many eyes belonging to beautiful faces;

Enjoying life & living to the fullest in every way;

I shall continue as best I can, no regrets, no shame, no guilt, no blame each day;

Loving all of creation as I have learned to love myself;

The freedom of my spirit shall not be placed upon a shelf.

In truth the right choices we make;

It is the lies that cause heart break;

Risks in life we are led to take;

If we choose not to take the chance, there is much as stake.

Love is Unity;

Unity is Divine will;

Divine will is Love . . .

And so the cycle of life continues . . . .

A note About the Author

This author has attended the school of life for almost 50 years. She has done research on numerous religions and various cultures, while with some participating or practicing the rituals or rites involved with them. She believes there are many Sages, whom have each left the knowledge their life experiences had brought, so others may learn and grow at their own pace. She does not display a degree in paper form upon a wall; she displays her degree in the life she lives and upon her soul.

Rita was born & primarily raised in central Midwestern United States. In staying close to her roots, she now resides in a simple country setting located next to a river in Minnesota. This has become her sanctuary, where she has come to understand herself as well as gaining an appreciation for nature at a deeper level. She is a practicing Spiritualist, opening up to the Master Creator and the creation of all that is around her. She spends her time with her children, granddaughter and with 3 four legged friends, considering all of them undoubtedly, her greatest blessings. She also enjoys traveling when time allows, living life to the fullest, enjoying every moment while experiencing all forms of nature, wondrous places and people.